Supporting Ordinary Schools

LEA initiatives

Supporting Ordinary Schools
LEA initiatives

Diana Moses,
Seamus Hegarty,
and
Sandra Jowett

NFER-NELSON

*Published by The NFER-NELSON Publishing Company Ltd.,
Darville House, 2 Oxford Road East,
Windsor, Berkshire SL4 1DF, England*

First Published 1988

*Typeset by First Page Ltd., Watford.
Printed by Billing & Sons Ltd., Worcester.*

*ISBN 0 7005 1177 6 (Hardback)
Code 8295 02 1*

*ISBN 0 7005 1163 6 (Paperback)
Code 8293 02 1*

Contents

The National Foundation for Educational Research

The National Foundation for Educational Research in England and Wales was founded in 1946 and is Britain's leading educational research institution. It is an independent body undertaking research and development projects on issues of current interest in all sectors of the public educational system. Its membership includes all the local education authorities in England and Wales, the main teachers' associations, and a large number of other major organizations with educational interests.

Its approach is scientific, apolitical and non-partisan. By means of research projects and extensive field surveys it has provided objective evidence on important educational issues for the use of teachers, administrators, parents and the research community. The expert and experienced staff that has been built up over the years enables the Foundation to make use of a wide range of modern research techniques, and, in addition to its own work, it undertakes a large number of specially sponsored projects at the request of government departments and other agencies.

The major part of the research programme relates to the maintained educational sector – primary, secondary and further education. A further significant element has to do specifically with local education authorities and training institutions. The current programme includes work on the education of pupils with special needs, monitoring of pupil performance, staff development, national evaluation and major curriculum programmes, test development, and information technology in schools. The Foundation is also the national agency for a number of international research and information exchange networks.

The NFER-NELSON Publishing Company are the main publishers of the Foundation's research reports. These reports are now available in the *NFER Research Library*, a collection which provides the educational community with up-to-date research into a wide variety of subject areas. In addition, the Foundation and NFER-NELSON work closely together to provide a wide range of open and closed educational tests and a test advisory service. NFER-NELSON also publish *Educational Research*, the termly journal of the Foundation.

Acknowledgements

The authors would like to thank all those people who completed the questionnaires sent to local education authorities. They provided us with detailed information about provision in their area and their help is much appreciated. We are grateful, too, to the education officers, advisers, educational psychologists, staff in the support services, headteachers and teachers who made themselves available for interview and contributed a great deal to our research. The comments and support of members of the Steering Committee were also of assistance.

We benefited greatly from constructive advice received from Fred Adams and George Cooke. Finally, we wish to acknowledge the assistance received from our colleagues at the National Foundation for Educational Research: Andy Stillman and Penelope Weston who made valuable suggestions on an earlier draft; David Upton who provided meticulous help with re-drafting; and Moci Carter and Jane Lever who supplied competent secretarial support.

1 Background and Introduction to the Research

Background

Special educational needs have now been in the educational spotlight for a period approaching ten years. The Warnock Report, published in 1978, not only represented a landmark in special education but also had a considerable impact on the rest of the education system. Many of its key recommendations are now enshrined in the Education Act 1981, which was implemented in April 1983. The DES-funded research project, 'Meeting Special Educational Needs: Support for the Ordinary School', began in the following autumn and was concluded three years later in 1986. Its focus of attention was on the range of strategies that enable ordinary schools to provide for all, or at any rate the great majority of their pupils, whatever their special needs may be. Meeting special needs is a more wide-ranging commitment than the implementation of legislation, and although the Act formed an important background to the study, the investigation centred upon policies and practices in schools and local authorities whether or not they were the direct result of legislation.

Three aspects of the Warnock Report were particularly influential in determining the ways in which special education would develop. First, it established the principle of the desirability of educating pupils with special needs as far as possible in ordinary schools. This principle has not subsequently been seriously challenged. Secondly, the abandonment of the established categories of handicap moved attention away from a concentration on what children with special needs could not do and the ways in which they were lacking, to an emphasis on their abilities and potential combined with an assessment of their individual special needs and provision to meet those needs. Thirdly, the new concept of special educational need was seen to apply not just to the two per cent of pupils who attended special schools but to an estimated 20 per cent of pupils, the vast majority of whom were in ordinary schools but for a variety of reasons were not flourishing. So, at the same time as a small number of pupils ceased to be categorized as handicapped, many more came to be regarded as being in need of special provision.

Although the Warnock Report was, without doubt, influential, its claims and recommendations were neither totally original nor unexpected. In many respects, it articulated the thinking that lay behind developments in provision that took place during the 1970s. Its recommendations came out of a climate of opinion which was already well established and can be traced back at least as far as 1970 when all children, including those previously 'regarded as unsuitable for education in school' and therefore the responsibility of local health authorities, became the responsibility of the local education authorities and thereby entitled to an education.

By 1980 many education officers felt that the Warnock Report had still not directly resulted in any major changes within their authorities, and considered that their policies had largely been determined by the same climate of opinion which had also produced the Report. At the time of its publication, many authorities were in the process of initiating certain integration programmes, particularly in the form of moving pupils from special schools into units attached to ordinary schools. The education officer from a county authority spoke for many of his colleagues when he said: 'Policy in relation to special education did not change dramatically, but Warnock gave a definite boost to things that were already happening and focussed more attention on special education. More interest generally is taken in this area of education, especially by the Education Committee.' Special educational provision became a subject for popular concern.

Many other local education authorities made a direct response to Warnock. A common course of action was the establishment of a new special needs working party or committee with a membership drawn from the elected members, education officers, the advisory service, the school psychological service and sometimes other support services, plus representatives from local voluntary organizations concerned with children and adults with special needs. These committees were frequently influential in the formulation of policy in the late 1970s and have continued to be central to the authorities' schemes for the implementation of the Act and the associated development of provision. Where these special needs committees have continued to operate, they have frequently been joined by staff from both ordinary and special schools and by representatives from health authorities and social services departments, thus constituting the first multi-disciplinary bodies which are well placed to play a key role in developing special needs provision in accordance with the terms of the Act.

When first constituted, the special needs committees were, through recommendations made to their education committees, often responsible for determining the whole nature and direction of future developments. It was in this way that many authorities decided to make important new appointments, especially of educational psychologists, special educational needs advisers, education officers and administrative support staff. These new staff played an important part in the implementation of the Act, but many of them were in post long before April 1983 and had been appointed at a time when it was still uncertain whether any of the recommendations of the Warnock Report would be given legislative force. It is clear that there was considerable activity in the local education authorities to improve provision for pupils with special educational needs well before the 1981 Act was on the statute book.

The moves towards integration can be seen as belonging to the same tradition of reform of the education system that first established secondary education for all, and later introduced comprehensive secondary schooling. All these reforms were based on the same basic principle that the best educational opportunities should be offered to the greatest number of children. Integration can be seen as an extension of opportunity to a group of children who had previously been denied it.

But, at the same time as the principle of integration calls for more pupils to be educated together in the same schools, the concept of special educational needs demands increased individualization of the curriculum within these schools. Ordinary schools must not simply accept a wider range of pupils than before; they have also to make appropriate provision for them. The changes that are thus required of schools inevitably make considerably heavier demands on them.

Other major changes in education, such as universal secondary education, the spread of comprehensive secondary schooling and the raising of the school leaving age, were all achieved in a climate of expansion. In some instances, expansion was an essential aspect of the innovation, but all took place when the number of children in the education system was increasing and were accompanied by increased spending on education. The drive towards greater integration is taking place at a time of economic stringency and also at a time when the total number of children of school age is declining. Many schools are experiencing falling rolls, and the associated problems make innovation particularly difficult to achieve. It was explicitly stated that no new funds would be made available for the implementation of the Education Act 1981, although it was expected to accomplish major changes.

In 1981 a study of special educational needs in primary schools found that the majority of headteachers felt that economies in the education service had resulted in a decline in the quality and quantity of provision they were able to offer pupils with special needs (Croll and Moses, 1985). They considered the main cause of this to be a decline in the number of part-time teachers available to schools for general teaching purposes, rather than a direct decrease in remedial or other special needs provision. Because of the common practice in primary schools of using part-time staff for special needs work, the effect of this economy was to make a substantial impact on special needs provision.

The same study reported that junior class teachers were of the opinion that nearly half their pupils whom they regarded as having special needs were not getting the help they needed. So, at a time when the new Act said that schools must identify and make appropriate provision for children with special educational needs, teachers felt that their ability to cater for these children had actually been reduced.

The special schools, too, were experiencing the problems of falling rolls in a particularly acute form. They were generally small institutions where even a slight decline in numbers could cause concern, especially when the school was already fearful for its future. Furthermore, special school staff were often concerned with maintaining pupil numbers, not just out of self-interest, but because they felt that the special school offered better opportunities for children with severe difficulties and that a fall in the school roll would mean that fewer of these children would receive the special provision they needed. In these circumstances, it is not surprising that the process of integration took time to gather momentum.

This may well be one of several reasons why the number of pupils in special schools has not substantially declined. During the late 1970s and early 1980s there had been a prevailing assumption, frequently expressed in the literature, that increasing numbers of children with special educational needs were being integrated into ordinary schools and that, correspondingly, the placement of children in special schools was declining. However, this assumption was strongly challenged by Swann (1985), who, using published DES figures, demonstrated that in the period 1978–82, although the absolute number of children in special schools fell, the decline was not as great as the overall fall in school numbers and that, consequently, the proportion of school-age children placed in special schools actually increased. This period was, of course, prior to the implementation of the 1981 Act and is not relevant to its operation. Nevertheless, there was a general assumption that the Warnock Report and the Act incorporated much of what was, in fact, rapidly spreading current practice.

More recent DES figures (GB. DES, 1986) seem to indicate that this may not in fact be the case. Between 1976 and 1984 the total school population fell by 12.5 per cent, but the special school population by only 7.2 per cent. However, the figures for the period 1983–84 show possible indications of a new trend: the number of special school pupils declined by 3.7 per cent over this period, whereas the total school population fell by only 2.1 per cent. Since the school population started to decline, this is the first year in which the special school population has shown a proportionally greater fall than the total school population.

It is difficult to state with accuracy how and why new special needs policies and practices originate. Trying to differentiate between the effects of the actual implementation of the Act, the influence of the Warnock Report, and the climate of opinion that formed the background to both is extremely problematic. Additionally, DES policies that do not have legislative force are nevertheless still likely to be influential, as are a whole variety of local factors that have resulted in very varied provision in the past and which continue to exert influence. In many instances, the origins of an innovation are likely to lie in a combination of several if not all of these factors. In some instances, however, it is possible to identify more precisely the factors which were most influential in shaping policy and practice. There can be little doubt, for example, that without the legal obligation few authorities would have introduced the Statementing procedures in their present form.

The research

This was the background against which the current research project – 'Meeting Special Educational Needs – Support for the Ordinary School' – was set when it began in the autumn of 1983. The study grew directly out of previous research into integration and provision for slow learners in ordinary schools carried out in recent years at the NFER (Hegarty and Pocklington, 1981, 1982; Clunies-Ross and Wimhurst, 1983; Hodgson *et al.*, 1984). A key theme emerging from this work and from both public and professional debate was that of support for the ordinary school. Despite the consensus of opinion about the desirability of maximum integration and the legal imperative that requires it, success will be difficult to achieve unless there is adequate support for the ordinary school. Integration has far-reaching resource implications, yet no new resources were made available by central government for the implementation of the Act. In these circumstances the strategies adopted by the local education authorities are of particular interest.

A major requirement of current developments in special education is that ordinary schools substantially improve and expand their provision for pupils with special needs, both for the relatively small number of pupils who become the subject of Statements and for the much larger number of pupils, mostly with mild learning difficulties or behavioural problems, that ordinary schools have always catered for, even if not always very satisfactorily.

The current research project investigated three distinct but interrelated areas in which ordinary schools could be helped in their task of providing appropriate education for all their pupils whatever their special educational needs. These three areas were the provision made by local education authorities, particularly in the form of support services; the establishment of links between special and ordinary schools; and the development of in-service training for teachers of pupils with special educational needs.

In the spring of 1984 a questionnaire seeking background information concerning all three major areas of interest was sent to each local education authority. Information was sought on special school and unit provision and the establishment of schemes linking special to ordinary schools; the extent of extra-district placements; changes in the staffing levels of the school psychological service and the advisory service; the establishment of designated special needs posts in ordinary schools; the operation of in-service training related to special needs; the special education budget; and the range of support services run by the authority.

Questionnaires were returned by 77 authorities, as indicated in Table 1.1. One of the difficulties of obtaining information in this field was the changing nature of the provision, and a number of the authorities which did not complete our questionnaire felt unable to do so because they were in the process of a major reorganization. It has not been possible to keep all the information collected fully up to date, but some action has been taken to ensure that as far as possible the data presented reflect the situation in 1986. Authorities that did not initially respond were not approached subsequently, but those which indicated that changes were imminent or in progress were contacted again and the data amended where necessary.

Table 1.1: *Questionnaires completed by the different types of local education authority*

Type of LEA	*Number*	*Number of questionnaires returned*	*%*
County	47	36	77
Metropolitan	36	25	69
London Boroughs (including ILEA)	21	16	76
All LEAs	104	77	74

On the basis of the information contained in the replies to the questionnaire, it was decided to pursue the three areas of interest separately. Further survey data were obtained on the operation of local education authority support services to assist both pupils with learning difficulties in ordinary schools and their teachers, from each of the 77 responding authorities. Similar data were obtained from 38 authorities operating services for the hearing impaired, and 24 authorities running services for the visually impaired. In addition, interviews were conducted with education officers, advisers, educational psychologists, members of the support services, headteachers and class teachers from a range of education authorities, often over a period of time, as new developments were being established.

The other two areas of interest – links between special schools and ordinary schools, and in-service training – were also the subject of further detailed enquiries, based on questionnaire surveys and case studies. These findings are reported in the companion volumes *Joining Forces: a study of links between special and ordinary schools* (Jowett, Hegarty and Moses, 1988), and *Developing Expertise: INSET for special educational needs* (Hegarty and Moses, 1988).

2 The Education Act 1981 and Ordinary Schools

Needs and provision

This chapter considers those aspects of the 1981 Act that directly affect ordinary schools, and in particular the allocation of resources that ordinary schools need to provide for pupils with a wide range of special educational needs. First, it is necessary to review some of the major elements of the Act and the various interpretations that can be made of particular clauses.

The Warnock Report, which formed the basis for much of the Act, recommended abandoning the term 'handicap' and the ten statutory categories, and introduced instead the term 'special educational need'. The concepts of 'handicap' and 'disability' relate primarily to the individual characteristics of the child or adult and imply that he or she is disadvantaged in significant areas of life, without in any way pointing towards a solution: 'To describe someone as handicapped conveys nothing of the type of educational help and hence provision that is required' (Warnock Report, 3:6).

The Report quoted a study by Webb, carried out in 1967, which used the term 'special educational need' and defined need in terms of provision: 'A study of an infants school in a good residential area in England found that of the 500 children who left the school over a six year period' 16 per cent needed some *additional help or consideration* on account of learning, behaviour or emotional problems' (our italics) (Warnock Report, 3:13). One of the major, and now very familiar recommendations of the Report was that 'the planning of services for children and young people should be based on the assumption that about one in six children at any time, and up to one in five children at some time during their school career will require some form of 'special educational provision'. In rejecting the concept of handicap and introducing special educational needs, Warnock brought together 'needs' and 'provision' and defined one in terms of the other, so that the child with special educational needs was the child who needed special provision. There was no retreating from this position; from that point onwards, needs and provision were inextricably linked.

The 1981 Act also defines special educational needs in terms of provision. Section 1(1) considers that a child has special educational needs if 'he has a learning difficulty which calls for special educational provision to be made for him' and goes on to specify that a child of statutory school age has a learning difficulty if:

(*a*) he has a significantly greater difficulty in learning than the majority of children of his age; or,

(*b*) he has a disability which either prevents or hinders him from making use of educational facilities of a kind generally provided in schools within the area of the local authority concerned, for children of his age. (section 1(2))

The Act does not explicitly address the question of the number of children who might need such provision. It appears, however, from DES Circular 8/81 (GB. DES, 1981) which followed the Act, that the estimate of 20 per cent proposed in the Warnock Report is accepted, together with the associated definition of special educational provision as encompassing 'the whole range and variety of additional help, whether it is provided on a full- or part-time basis, by which children may be helped to overcome educational difficulties, however they are caused' (Warnock Report, 3:38).

The concept of 'extra' provision

It would appear that the Act is calling for a very considerable amount of 'extra' or 'additional' help for a large number of children, but the notions of what can properly be regarded as extra, and to what exactly the additional provision is extra, remains problematic. Later on, the process of Statementing – the decision by a local authority to accept direct responsibility for a child's special educational needs – and the resulting allocation of resources will be considered. It is clear that all children with special needs, by definition, require extra provision, yet the nature of this provision and the responsibility for providing it are unclear for children without Statements. Some indications are given: section 4 of the Act, which deals with the duty of the authority to identify children with special needs, makes a distinction between 'those with special educational needs which call for the *LEA to determine the special educational provision* that should be made for them' and other children (our italics). For the most part, those children identified under section 4 will become the subject of Statements under section 7, in which the LEA makes a statement of needs and provision.

The question of provision for children who are not afforded the protection of a Statement is dealt with under section 2(5) which lays duties upon school governors.

> It shall be the duty of the governors . . .
> (*a*) to use their best endeavours, in exercising their functions in relation to the school, to secure that if any registered pupil has special educational needs the special educational provision that is required for him is made;
> (*b*) to ensure that, where the responsible person has been informed by the LEA that a registered pupil has special educational needs, those needs are made known to all who are likely to teach him; and
> (*c*) to ensure that the teachers in the school are aware of the importance of identifying, and providing for, those registered pupils who have special educational needs.

It is of significance that this duty is not an absolute one and the expression used is 'best endeavours'. As Cox, in his commentary on the Act, points out: 'Presumably the expression "best endeavours" really means best endeavours within the financial resources available since the Act is not intended to have resource implications and since the governors do not determine the financial resources available to them' (Cox, 1985). In these circumstances it would be extremely difficult to establish that 'best endeavours' had not been used. The result is that much of the provision for children with special educational needs is provided at the discretion of ordinary schools, frequently without additional financial resources.

It is clear that the legislation expects that much of the 'extra' provision will be arranged both by individual schools and services without the use of statutory procedures. In relation to the assessment of needs, paragraph 15 of DES Circular 1/83 (GB. DES, 1983) states that 'formal procedures are not required where ordinary schools provide special educational provision from their own resources in the form of additional or remedial provision, or, in normal circumstances where the child attends a reading centre or unit for disruptive pupils'. However, such extra provision, whether provided from the school's resources or not, must fall within the definition of special educational provision contained in section 1 of the Act – 'provision not made generally for children . . . in schools, maintained by the local education authority'. The important question is whether or not the provision is made generally available in the authority concerned.

It seems doubtful whether the help that can be offered in the classroom by the class teacher, however effective it may be, can ever be regarded as 'extra'. A particular programme of work may indeed be highly beneficial and may be different from, or indeed extra to, the work previously done, but in the context of ongoing work in the classroom it is difficult to see how it can be regarded as extra provision. It is very questionable whether special educational provision can, or should ever be incorporated fully into the ordinary working of the classroom, provided by and accepted as the responsibility of the class teacher in the primary school and subject teachers in the secondary school. The arguments here, are in many ways similar to those concerning the integration of the administration of ordinary and special education. The case for an integrated administration and the case for the class teacher having responsibility for special provision in schools are both, in many respects, compelling. In practice, however, it is easy to see that in both cases a separation of function and responsibility could result not in the real amalgamation of ordinary and special, but in the virtual disappearance of the special.

Nevertheless, teachers in ordinary schools clearly have a crucial part to play. A recent survey of junior school teachers found that class teachers do consider that the ordinary classroom is the right place for the vast majority of pupils with special educational needs to spend most of their time in school, and that they are prepared to take responsibility for them. The same survey also found that most of the teachers in the study had little or no training in teaching children with special needs or in the teaching of reading (Croll and Moses, 1985). Gipps *et al.*, made a study of provision in primary schools in 1985 and reported an increase in the number of primary school teachers who had received in-service training, but there still remained a very substantial number of teachers with no training in this field (Gipps *et al.*, 1987).

The Act itself makes no direct reference to in-service training but the associated DES Circular 1/83 states that 'the Secretary of State for Education and Science expects that the LEAs will encourage in-service training to assist teachers in recognizing and meeting special educational needs'. Very few people would argue against the desirability of more in-service training, which is almost certain to improve the quality of provision in the classroom for children with special needs, just as it is likely to improve the teaching of English, maths or whatever. However, teachers are under increasing pressure to take on a whole range of initiatives and it is difficult to see how they can do justice to them all. It is also unclear whether the improved classroom practice that hopefully results from training can be regarded as the 'extra' or 'additional' provision required by the Act. It is of significance in this context that the teachers in the study by Gipps *et al.*, though favourably disposed to receiving further training, did not see it as the best way to provide for children with special educational needs and did not regard what they themselves did as constituting extra provision.

Central to the concept of extra provision is the difficult issue of what is 'generally available in schools'. The provision that the class teacher can make for pupils as the result of in-service training may not be extra provision, but it can make a significant difference to what is generally available in schools. It can also alter the baseline of provision upon which further provision is built.

Although the Act encompasses the whole of Warnock's 20 per cent, it is clearly intended that there should be differentiation within that 20 per cent. Provision for the majority of these pupils is to be left to the 'best endeavours' of the governors of individual schools, with support in a variety of forms, – for example, in-service training, LEA support services, and designated posts to be provided by the local authority. This range of provision is described and discussed in subsequent chapters. However, the Act also requires more formalized procedures and more substantial and wide-ranging help and support for some pupils, and it is the identification, assessment and statement of provision for these children that is at the heart of the Act.

The definition of special educational needs in the Act, with the emphasis placed on the close connection between needs and provision, has clear resource implications. The broad intentions of the Act apply equally to all LEAs but there remains the possibility of considerable variation between authorities in the level of provision they maintain. There are marked differences between authorities in the 'generally available level of provision', and in the number of children that they decide require provision over and above this level, as well as in the types and locations of schools in which the children receive special educational provision. The following pages consider those duties of LEAs which have most relevance to the allocation of resources to ordinary schools.

The duty to educate in ordinary schools

Section 2 of the 1981 Act deals with one of the most widely known aspects of the legislation – the duty to educate in ordinary schools. The Act requires that LEAs should educate children with special educational needs in ordinary schools, but only if certain conditions are met. These conditions are laid out in section 2(3) of the Act and specify that the authority must ensure that the views of parents are taken into account and that educating the child in an ordinary school is compatible with '(*a*) his receiving the special educational provision that he requires; (*b*) that provision of efficient education for the children with whom he will be educated; and (*c*) the efficient use of resources'.

It is not unusual for commentators on the Act to regard these conditions as 'escape clauses' which get the education authorities off the hook and mean, in effect, that the Act has no real power to force authorities to pursue integrationist policies (Galloway, 1985). Without these provisos the Act would, of course, be much 'stronger' but, particularly in the short and medium term, their omission would make it much more difficult and perhaps impossible to implement. The provisos do not preclude authorities working towards a situation where all children are educated in ordinary schools. Secondly, implicit in the commentaries of Galloway and others is the firmly held, but largely unsubstantiated, belief that LEAs are opposed to change and reluctant to implement the Act. When the steps that the authorities have taken to implement the Act are looked at in more detail, this appears to be a very difficult position to hold. Leaving the actual legislation aside there were very few, if any, authorities who did not respond positively to the Warnock Report. Croll and Moses (1985) found that in 1980 the ten authorities in which they conducted their research all responded with the establishment of working parties to review policy and practice, and were in the process of introducing changes in 'the spirit of Warnock' in advance of the legislation. For instance, the Special Needs Action Programme in Coventry was established in 1982 following a considerable period of planning.

It should be appreciated, too, that integration is not a new, exclusively post-Warnock phenomenon. Pupils with special needs of all types and various degrees of severity had been educated in ordinary schools for many years, but unfortunately there are no figures available on these children. The process of ascertainment which was replaced under the Act by multi-professional assessment and Statementing was essentially ascertainment for special school placements, and the placement of children with special needs in ordinary schools was not recorded systematically. Nevertheless some indication that the presence of children with special needs in junior classrooms was not unusual is provided by Croll and Moses (1985). A vast majority of the class teachers in their study had at some time taught children whose disabilities were such that placement in a special school could be considered a reasonable alternative.

There are other positive indications of seriousness of intent on the part of the LEAs in relation to implementing the Act. Most authorities created new posts, both in the education office and in schools, expressly to implement the Act and to create the type of provision encouraged by Warnock. Details of the range of new posts of Education Officer for Special Educational Needs, additional posts in the school psychological service and other support services, newly created posts of Adviser for Special Educational Needs and designated posts in schools, are discussed in later chapters.

An important feature of the 'escape clauses' is that, in contrast to many of the provisions of the Act, they are expressed in objective language. As Cox (1985) points out, this means that an authority is not entitled simply to say: 'This is our decision and there are reasonable grounds for reaching such a decision'. In the case of the decision to carry out or refuse a multi-professional assessment, that is the situation and so it is very difficult to challenge. By contrast, the 'escape clauses' are not at the discretion of the authority and are open to challenge by parents and others.

In section 2 (7), addressing the duty to integrate, the Act provides that,

> Where a child who has special educational needs is being educated in an ordinary school maintained by the LEA it shall be the duty of those concerned with making special educational provision for that child to secure, as far as is both compatible with the objectives mentioned in paragraphs (*a*) to (*c*) of subsection (3) above [i.e. 'the escape clauses'] and *reasonably practicable*, that the child engages in the activities of the school together with children who do not have special educational needs.

Again 'reasonably practicable' means that the judgement of the LEA can be challenged.

Assessments and Statements

Although the Act covers the whole 20 per cent of pupils considered by the Warnock Report to have special needs, it also follows the recommendations of that Report in regarding a much smaller number of children differently, ensuring that their particular needs for special educational provision are protected in law. The Warnock Report recommended that 'there should be a system of recording as in need of special educational provision those children who, on the basis of a detailed profile of their needs prepared by a multi-professional team, are judged by their local education authority to require special educational provision not generally available in ordinary schools'(3:31). An estimate of the number of children to whom this would apply was approximately two per cent – the same proportion of the school age population which was at that time in special schools and units.

The Act, in sections 4 to 7, gives legislative force to the recommendations of the Warnock Committee relating to the identification and assessment of children with special educational needs. The Act itself gives no very positive direction about the numbers of children who should be the subject of either multi-professional assessments or Statements, but some guidance is offered in the DES Circulars, and education authorities implementing the Act can also refer to Warnock. In DES Circular 8/81, paragraph 9 declares that:

> The Secretary of State will expect LEAs to afford children the protection of a statement of their special educational needs in all circumstances where extra resources in terms of staffing or equipment would be required to cater for those needs in ordinary schools. It is expected that *the number will correspond approximately to those children formerly ascertained as handicapped under Section 34 of the 1944 Act* (our italics).

Later DES Circular 1/83 says,

> As a general rule, the Secretary of State expects LEAs to afford the protection of a statement to all children who have severe or complex learning difficulties which require the provision of extra resources in ordinary schools, a special school, a non-maintained special school, or an independent school approved for the purpose.

This is as much help as is given. It is clear that an assessment and a Statement are required for pupils in special schools, but whether or not a Statement is required for pupils in ordinary schools depends on a judgement about whether or not they require additional resources. This, in turn, is obviously dependent upon the current type and level of provision, which varies both between and within authorities and is itself difficult to determine. In these circumstances it is not surprising that authorities differ both in their interpretation of the law and its implementation.

LEA policies on Statementing

It is possible for an authority to write no Statements for children in ordinary schools. It is equally possible for Statements to be written for every child who receives any additional help such as that provided by support services or a reading centre. Although in reality these very extreme positions are unlikely to be taken, policies do vary very widely indeed. It is doubtful whether there is any authority which has no children with Statements in ordinary schools, but there are those which have very few. However, the level of Statementing gives no clear indications of the amount of integration taking place. This can be illustrated by the policies and practices of four education authorities.

One county authority adopted a policy of never writing Statements for children in ordinary schools, and this remained the policy of the authority, although there were exceptions in individual cases, such as children who were on the roll of a special school but who actually received much of their education in an ordinary school. This authority was not opposed to the education of pupils with special needs in ordinary schools and was not attempting to undermine the Act. In fact, it was one of the pioneers in integration, with many successful schemes originating well before the publication of the Warnock Report. Largely because of its history of integration and relatively generous education resources, the chief education officer argued that no child needed the protection of a Statement because he or she would never be placed in a school that could not offer a proper level of provision. There were additional advantages in a low level of Statementing, he felt, because fewer multi-professional assessments would have to be conducted and these were very demanding of time and skilled manpower. The authority could act within the law by preparing Statements only for children in special schools and still actively pursue its previous policy of integration.

Warnock had previously pointed out the dangers inherent in this situation:

> Unless these needs and the corresponding means of meeting them are explicitly recorded there will be a real danger of insufficiency or default in their provision. Secondly, even though regular specialist help may be available to the ordinary school which a child is currently attending there can be no guarantee, in the absence of a formulation of need and provision, that it will continue to be available if he moves to another school, whether in the same area or that of another local authority (Warnock Report, 4:69).

These dangers are very real in practice and highlight the desirability of Statements to protect the interests of children. It would be particularly advantageous for a child with a serious disability in an ordinary school in this authority to have a Statement of his or her needs and provision in case he or she should move to a neighbouring authority with a different policy. In these circumstances the child might be unable to find a place in a suitable school, and even placement in a special school would not be without its difficulties in the absence of a multi-professional assessment and a Statement.

In another low Statementing authority, policy and practice were both very different. The writing of very few Statements for children in ordinary schools was virtually their only similarity. This authority had a history of extensive special school placement, much of it in the form of 'extra-district' placements. Over the last few years the use made of special schools outside the authority had been considerably reduced. This policy was adopted in many authorities, often for both philosophical and economic reasons. It was frequently the case that the money saved by a reduction in such placements could be used to establish new and/or expanded services to support ordinary schools educating pupils with special educational needs. In this particular authority such a reorganization was not possible, even if the desire had been there, because the money saved on the 'extra-district' placements was regarded as a saving made by the local authority as a whole, not as money saved by one sector of education that could be the subject of virement within the education department. For the most part, the children who would previously have been placed in schools outside the county were placed instead in special schools maintained by the authority.

The position of the authority was that while in principle it favoured the integration of children with special educational needs and was striving to implement the Act, it was also very aware of the resource implications. It argued that in the current climate of restriction and economy it was impossible to supply 'extra' in ordinary schools when there were places available in special schools. The policy of the authority was that 'extra' provision could only be made in special schools, although exceptions to this general rule could be made in individual cases. Most of the children being educated in ordinary schools had severe physical handicaps but were of average or above average intellectual ability. No schools in the authority were adapted, or provided with special facilities for pupils with physical handicaps. The integration of these pupils was in the form of individual placements, and arrangements were made on an ad hoc basis. This did not mean that they were necessarily unsatisfactory for those involved, but it did indicate that these placements did not form part of an organized policy. There were no pupils of junior school age or older in the county's ordinary schools who were the subject of Statements because of behaviour problems or moderate learning difficulties; these special needs were always met in special schools and units. All these factors indicate a very different situation from the previous authority in relation to making provision for special educational needs, yet both had very few pupils with Statements in ordinary schools.

Although the attitude of the authority towards meeting special needs, the resources that are available and the skill with which they are administered all have considerable impact on the level of Statements, the existing level of provision in ordinary schools is probably of paramount importance. Especially relevant here is the support that can be provided by the support services. (The range and variety of work carried out by the support services are described in later chapters.) The following examples serve to illustrate how different levels of support service provision can affect policy and practice in relation to the writing of Statements for children in ordinary schools.

One of the largest LEAs is a county with a history of substantial special school provision and, unusually, no remedial reading service. To assist in the implementation of the Act, the authority made a number of new appointments but did not establish a special needs support service. As the policy of the authority was to implement the Act 'in the spirit of Warnock' and educate children with special educational needs in ordinary schools, the result was the writing of Statements for a large number of children with mild learning difficulties and specific reading problems. For each of these children a full multi-professional assessment was carried out, and if the extra provision required necessitated additional teaching time, as it usually did, this was provided by the appointment of a temporary, part-time teacher appointed to the school that the child attended. This policy resulted in a large number of children in ordinary schools with Statements, but did not necessarily lead to a decrease in the number of children in special schools, as many of the children with Statements would not be afforded this protection in some other authorities, because their needs would be met by the support services and this help would be regarded as falling within 'what is usually available in schools maintained by the authority'.

This was the case in a neighbouring authority which adopted a very different approach, largely as the result of very different provision being available. Here, children with mild learning difficulties and specific reading difficulties received help from the special educational needs advice and support service, which had a staff of nearly 80, who were able to offer assistance to large numbers of children and their teachers. These children received help inaddition to that which was generally available in the classroom from the staff of the school, but not additional to that generally available in the authority.

Thus, many children who have the protection of a Statement in one authority may well not have it in another. In authorities that operate special needs support services – the vast majority – it can be difficult to decide whether a child who receives considerable assistance from the support service should be given the protection of a Statement. It can be argued that where this type of help forms part of the established provision it is unnecessary to write a Statement, and that the whole process of carrying out multi-professional assessments and producing Statements is very wasteful of resources that could be better used in other ways to support the child and his/her teacher. But clearly there are dangers in this approach. The provision may be insufficient, and even where it is fully adequate, there is no guarantee that it will continue to be so. A Statement does guarantee by law that the child gets the stated type and level of provision; all other arrangements are at the discretion of the LEA and are subject to changes in policy and financial stringency.

A compromise solution adopted by some authorities in this situation has been to adopt a system of 'named' children. A 'named' child is one that is guaranteed a declared amount of special provision by the LEA, but the guarantee does not carry the weight of law. Nevertheless, this guarantee can be regarded as more than a mere promise. First, it should be remembered that authorities are using their 'best endeavours' to make adequate provision and are not wilfully trying to evade their responsibilities. Secondly, this system is operated by the school psychological service or special needs support service which is likely to be in a position to ensure adequate provision and to take the decision that a multi-professional assessment should be made if this proves to be necessary. An additional merit of this system is the increased speed and flexibility it gives. Because the procedures for 'naming' a child are much quicker and simpler than for writing a Statement, children who need intensive help over a short period of time are much more easily catered for.

Assessment procedures in the ordinary school

Some children will enter school with Statements as a result of a multi-professional assessment having been carried out before they reach school age. However, many children will first have their special needs identified in the classroom of an ordinary school. This is particularly likely in the case of mild and moderate learning difficulties, specific reading problems and behavioural problems, though other special needs may also be recognized first in the ordinary school.

Section 2(5) of the 1981 Act, already quoted, makes it the duty of school governors 'to secure that the teachers in the school are aware of the importance of identifying, and providing for those registered pupils who have special educational needs'. Section 4, on the duty to identify children with special needs, makes it quite clear that, although 20 per cent of children may have special needs that require provision, it is the much smaller group of approximately two per cent that require very special attention. Here the Act calls upon the LEAs, not the governors of schools, to identify 'those with special educational needs which call for the LEA to determine the special educational provision that should be made for them'. Although there is inevitably a grey area in the middle, it appears that the school has a duty (presumably with the assistance of support services) to identify and provide for pupils for whom it is possible for them to provide, within the normal range of provision, and the education authority has a duty to identify those pupils whose special needs are such that they require a Statement. It is the education authority, and not the governors or the headteachers of the schools attended by the children in question, which is responsible for identification, because the educational psychologists and the other professionals involved in the identification, assessment and Statementing process work as agents of the authority and not for particular schools.

As Cox points out: '. . . it is important to appreciate that the key to all assessment and identification provisions of the Act is to be found in Section 7 which deals with the process of statementing. Identification and MPA (multi-professional assessment) are only intended to apply to children for whom statements are to be written so the nature of this process and particularly how many children and professionals are concerned will depend on the authority's policy towards statementing' (Cox, 1985).

For virtually all children with less severe problems, and for some children with severe and complex difficulties, identification will begin in the classroom. Warnock put forward a model for identification and assessment, and procedures along these lines have been adopted by most authorities. The process can be explained by taking the case of a nine-year-old in a primary school whose inability to read well enough to cope in the class is causing concern to his/her teacher. The first course of action for the teacher is to discuss the problem with the teacher responsible for special needs. This will often be a new post created by the local authority in response to the recommendations of Warnock. These two teachers will take the child through the school's own identification and assessment procedures and, together with the headteacher, decide whether or not the school can meet the child's special needs without any further assistance. If the decision is that the school can cope, the help given to the child will be what the class teacher him/herself can provide, together with the advice and support of the colleague with special responsibility for special needs and possibly also help from a 'remedial' teacher (if the school has one). It is the last type of help, withdrawal from the class for extra help with a remedial teacher, that the junior school teachers in the study by Croll and Moses regarded as particularly advantageous for children with learning and reading difficulties and would like to see offered to many more children (Croll and Moses, 1985).

This responsibility for early identification and provision may perhaps appear as an onerous additional task for schools, but it should be remembered that schools have always undertaken these activities and they have always been vitally important for the children concerned. What is new, in the wake of Warnock and the Act, is a more general awareness of these processes and their significance. This is reflected in the increased attention given to them by both the DES and the LEAs. Special educational needs in ordinary schools have been given top priority in in-service training as well as greater emphasis in initial teacher training.

After the schools' procedures have been completed, it may be decided that the child's needs are such that they cannot be met without additional outside help and/or advice. At this point, help from one of the advisory and support services will be sought. There are several ways in which this contact can be made, and the procedures vary greatly between different authorities and between different services in the same authority. Additionally, many support services have been subject to reorganization within the last five years and have modified, or sometimes radically changed the way they operate and the service they give. There can easily be uncertainty about the exact point at which the school should ask for help, who to ask and how to do it. These issues are dealt with in later chapters on the operation of the support services.

If, with the assistance of the support service involved, it is decided by the school and the support service that the child's needs can be met by the type of service that is routinely provided (usually a few hours' extra specialist teaching in a small group), then the child is still unlikely to be the subject of a multi-professional assessment.

The multi-professional assessment

Of central importance is the decision to begin the multi-professional assessment. Whoever makes this decision in effect decides whether it is appropriate to make a Statement. In principle, it is possible for the assessment and the Statementing to be quite separate processes, with many assessments not resulting in the writing of a Statement. The Act makes it clear that the two processes have distinct functions: that the assessment must deal with the child's needs in the opinions of professionals and parents, without reference to the provision available in the authority concerned; and the Statement is concerned with how the stated needs are going to be met. In practice, although there is concern to keep the two processes separate and not allow currently available and traditionally acceptable provision to pre-empt the assessment, it is unusual for multi-professional assessments not to result in Statements.

There are, however, some interesting exceptions in practice. The close connection between need and provision has been stressed, and inevitably provision is dependent on resources. In some circumstances it is possible for the multi-professional assessment to imply strongly the need for a type or level of provision which is not currently available in the authority. When this happens, the officer in charge of Statementing has a difficult decision to make. If the Statement is drawn up, the authority is under a legal obligation to make available the provision laid down in the document, which in some instances may be extremely costly – and may be considered inappropriate by senior officers or by elected members. On the other hand, the multi-professional assessment has involved the parents of the child and considerable time and work on the part of several professionals, of whom many, if not all, will be calling for action. It will be extremely difficult for the officer concerned to rule that the Statement is now inappropriate. A temporary solution may lie in delay, and there are instances of multi-professional assessments piling up in anticipation that at some point in the future it will be possible to secure the resources available to enable an appropriate Statement to be written.

The separation of assessment and Statement lies at the heart of the difference between the new process of securing special educational provision and the previous process of ascertainment for special educational treatment. As Welton *et al.* (1982) pointed out, under the former ascertainment procedures, 'although decisions about special educational needs could logically include adding extra resources to a child's present school situation, in practice most multi-professional assessment and decision making assumed that a child should be moved'. In practice, the process was one of ascertainment for a place in a special school or unit. The SE forms procedure would only be instigated after the school psychological service had consulted the child's school, the special school and the parents and there was general agreement that placement in special education was in the best interests of the child.

It is worth bearing in mind that, although parents have been granted more explicit rights of consultation under the Act than was previously the case, parents' wishes have always been taken into account. Most, if not all, LEAs operated a policy of requiring a school to secure parental consent before a child could be seen, even informally, by an educational psychologist and only in most unusual circumstances were parental wishes overridden. (Indeed, parental wishes can still be set aside.) Good practice was to consult fully and work with parents – as it is now. Assessment by the school psychological service could, and did, lead to children with a variety of needs remaining in the ordinary classroom, but the SE forms procedure would not be carried out for these children as they were not preparing to move into special schools. Under the 1981 Act the Statementing process secures a child special educational provision but not, of course, necessarily in a special school or unit.

Whatever stance the local authority may take, it risks being accused of pursuing policies on economic grounds to the detriment of both pupils and teachers. Provision in a separate sector of education is seen by many as a cheaper alternative to integration, while supporters of special schools see mainstream provision as a cheap, inferior option. Detailed comparative costings of different types of provision are extremely complex and rarely attempted.

So far, in considering the powers and actions of LEAs, it has been implied that it is the officers who represent the authority. Although it is usually the case that the officers do act in this way, in the last resort it is the elected members with whom power lies. The resource implications of implementing the Act are emphasized in those authorities where the elected members are directly concerned with the Statementing process. In some instances the draft Statement is presented to one of the education sub-committees for approval before further action can be taken. Refusing permission for the Statement to proceed would be an extreme action but it is one which elected members could take, although this decision could subsequently be appealed against by the parents. The involvement of the members can, it is claimed, serve to emphasize the significance of the Act, the resource implications of the legislation and the power that they can wield. Presenting draft Statements to elected members also draws to their attention the issues involved in special educational provision through the consideration of the needs of individual children. Officers in authorities who have adopted this policy feel that dealing with specific cases in this way encourages the members to see the need for adequate resources to meet special educational needs.

3 Budgeting for Special Educational Needs

This chapter presents a brief account of how local authorities manage their education budgets, with particular reference to the budgeting arrangements that are being, or could be made, to provide for pupils with special needs. There follows an account of one authority where significant changes in provision have been accomplished in the wake of Warnock and the Act within the constraints of a restricted budget.

Education is only one of the services provided by local government, although it is by far the biggest spender. Its share of the total council budget is not fixed but open to challenge, negotiation and change. Apart from local rates, the main source of revenue for local government is central government grants, of which the major portion is a general grant towards all county council expenditure – the rate support grant (RSG). In recent years, the proportion of total local government expenditure met from central government grants, as opposed to rates, has increased substantially. In addition to RSG, there are some specific central government grants for particular purposes – for example the police, and some elements in other budgets, such as the urban aid programme. It had been hoped that the implementation of the 1981 Act would have attracted such additional funding, but this has not proved to be the case. There has, however, been specific funding for in-service training, and special educational needs in ordinary schools is one of the priority areas.

Educational expenditure is determined locally, but is subject to monitoring and, ultimately, control by central government. Although more attention is now given to government direction, this is not a new phenomenon. Since the reorganization of local government in 1974, central government has indicated which items have been taken into account in fixing the RSG, although until fairly recently it accepted the principle of general grant and imposed no detailed constraints on the application of funds or limits on total expenditure. Authorities generally tried to follow the Government's Public Expenditure Survey guidelines as a defence against criticisms by the Government for over-spending, and from the recipients of services for inadequate standards. What is new in recent years is, first, the fixing of overall spending targets for local authorities with penalties exacted for over-spending, and secondly, the use of 'rate-capping' powers by central government to limit increases in locally-levied rate revenue. There has also been an increasing tendency towards specific grants to ensure that central government's priorities and policies are achieved. These measures have, on the whole, been very unpopular with the local authorities, since they restrict the scope of their own discretion to determine local policies and priorities in accordance with local needs and circumstances.

There are two main areas left for local determination: the distribution of resources between different services, and the distribution of resources within each service department. In all authorities, decisions have to be made to determine priorities among the various services – education, social services, public protection, leisure services, transportation and the environment – all competing for a share of scarce resources. There is nothing new about this problem, but in recent years the emphasis has been on an explicitly 'corporate' approach aiming ideally to achieve the best for the whole, rather than considering individual services independently. This, of course, involves the extremely difficult task of comparing the claims for money put forward by departments which are offering very different services; it becomes necessary to attempt a comparison and evaluation of the relative benefits to the community of money spent on extra teachers, more social workers or better roads. Such decisions are usually taken by some form of Policy and Resources Committee, which has the task of co-ordinating or overriding the interests of the various sectors. It is difficult to overestimate the power of this committee. Its influence is likely to be particularly strong in times of economic recession when extra money going to one service almost inevitably means cuts for another service.

The major significance of this situation for education is that, as the largest service, it is thereby expected to make the largest savings, sometimes with little regard for its statutory responsibilities and the very limited financial discretion that is left within the overall expenditure budget. When other services can implement schemes with sums of money that are relatively small in comparison with overall expenditure by the education service, it is sometimes tempting for the Policy and Resources Committee to satisfy the smaller demands of another department by savings made in a particular sector of education. This means that potential savings in education, through falling rolls, for example, which could be used to sustain and improve the level of provision, may be lost to education and gained by a competing service. There is, throughout local government, a very strong notion that an important aspect of managing any particular service is the attempt to secure more resources for it. Expanding the budget is no less important than deciding how to spend the resources already available.

The total budget for the education service, then, is not fixed and secure but often involves fierce competition. It may in some ways be convenient to think of the education budget as a cake that can be divided up in a variety of ways with a large slice for someone resulting in a smaller slice for someone else. But it must be borne in mind that there are other forces at work – some trying to enlarge the size of the cake and others attempting to reduce it.

Another area of local control is the distribution of resources within the service departments themselves. In the case of education, this involves apportionment between the competing claims of the various major sectors – schools, further education and special education – and also priorities within these areas, for example, youth and community services as opposed to technical colleges. When various alternative strategies for resource allocation are considered, it is important to realize that the bulk of the education budget allows for little manoeuvring. In a typical authority over 60 per cent of the budget comprises salaries and wages, while other items such as loan charges and mandatory grants are fixed, so that the opportunities for innovation within existing budget provision are very limited, as are opportunities for effecting economies.

Turning now to the particular problems of financing increased support for ordinary schools to help them provide for pupils with special educational needs, it is important to recognize that ordinary and special education have generally been regarded as separate enterprises, and the separation of the two systems has been reflected in separate budget headings. Special education was what happened in special schools and was the subject of distinct financial arrangements. Although there is considerable variation in relation to the items included within the special education budget, the headings presented below can be regarded as not untypical.

The special education budget

The budget includes all identifiable items of expenditure relating to special schools, special units, hospital schools, home tuition and the school psychological service. Special education items cover:

1 salaries and wages;
2 maintenance of premises, heating and lighting;
3 equipment, supplies and materials;
4 transport of pupils;
5 establishment expenses;
6 payment for special school places provided extra-district by other LEAs or at independent schools.

This list is in keeping with budgeting arrangements for what has traditionally been seen, to all intents and purposes, as a separate education system. Some contact can be seen with the mainstream through the school psychological service, which operates in both special and ordinary sectors. This overlap results in funding for the psychological service being found under a variety of headings in different authorities. Although the cost of the school psychological service is generally considered as a discrete unit, it may be a sub-heading under special education, as in the example presented here, or it may stand as a separate heading in its own right, or even be included in the school's budget. Other connections with mainstream provision are illustrated by milk and meals for special education being included in a general budget for these services and not appearing as a separate item.

At this point, the complications of budgeting for the range of provision in ordinary schools that could be regarded as special education – support services, advisers, adaptations to buildings, specialist equipment, specialist staff based in ordinary schools, non-teaching assistants and in-service education – become apparent. There is no obvious solution to this problem. The arrangements made vary according to individual local characteristics and practices, and to some extent the decisions may be arbitrary. It has been argued that policies of integration in schools should be administered by an integrated administration with a single budget, on the grounds that an administration that is divided between special and ordinary schools generates unnecessary conflicts. According to this line of argument, plans for integration should include combining the ordinary and special education budgets. However, this had not happened in any of the 77 authorities providing information for this study, and there were no plans to do so. In fact, there were instances of the reverse happening. Where, prior to Warnock and the Act, the special education budget had been combined with another, usually the primary schools budget, and the two jointly administered, increased activity in the field of special educational needs had more often resulted in a separation of the two budgets!

Since 1978 there has actually been a tendency to move more items into the special education budget if at all feasible. The reason for this appears to be the belief that when the authority is looking for economies, the special education budget is less likely to be a target, partly because the elected members will shy away from the emotive issue of reducing funds for pupils with special needs and partly because the much publicized and widely acclaimed Warnock Report and the 1981 Act have focused attention on special needs, making it an unpopular subject for cuts. This is well illustrated by the case of funding for the support services. Local authorities which operated the traditional type of remedial reading service usually funded this service from the primary sector of the schools budget. Several authorities have now transformed their remedial reading services along the lines recommended by Warnock into a special educational needs support service and others are likely to adopt this strategy. Alongside this reorganization has gone a change in accounting procedures, with the new services being located in the special education sector of the budget where there is less likelihood of cut-backs, and even the possibility of limited expansion.

Dalebridge and the budget – a strategy for change in one metropolitan authority

By considering one authority in more detail, it is possible to see how substantial changes can be brought about without additional spending. In this instance, policy development appears to have been initiated largely by the chief education officer, whose recommendations were generally endorsed by the Education Committee. Little consultation appears to have taken place, apart from a proposal for the reorganization of the remedial reading service which was circulated to all schools and service staff involved.

These proposals were presented in considerable detail and the time allowed for comments prior to their implementation was very brief. The reorganization was carried through with a fair degree of determination: no one was fired and everyone had their salaries protected, but several resignations and requests for early retirement were willingly accepted. The chief education officer saw the Act as an opportunity for a 'fresh start', and adopted a more radical approach than many other administrators. Generally, reorganization and change were achieved within the context of existing structures and personnel.

Responding to the Act

There were five key areas around which changes in provision for children with special needs were accomplished in Dalebridge:

1. the appointment of a new adviser for children with special educational needs;
2. the establishment of the Assessment and Learning Support Service;
3. the reorganization and later expansion of the school psychological service;
4. the creation and then expansion of a service for the hearing impaired;
5. the establishment of provision for children with speech impairment.

Like virtually every other LEA, Dalebridge had experienced falling rolls in its schools over the last decade. This created many problems, but did not open up the opportunities for the re-allocation of resources that might have been expected. In principle, as Warnock had argued, it seemed reasonable to suppose that falling rolls would release money in education budgets, enabling LEAs to finance various initiatives and improvements, and that special educational needs would be at or near the top of the list for this spare money. Unfortunately, the actual situation was very different.

In Dalebridge, for example, the proportion of the total local authority budget allocated to education was largely determined by pupil numbers, so that a decline in the school population resulted in a decline in the total revenue available to the education service. The money that had been saved potentially each year as numbers declined was returned to central funding, from where the education service could attempt to recover it by bidding for its return. But education was in direct competition for this money with the other local government services. It was not in any way in a privileged position. This left the education department with all the problems created by falling rolls, but none of the associated advantages of being able to re-allocate the monies saved. It was against this background that the financing of the educational changes required or encouraged by the Act had to be considered. In addition, it should be noted that even where money saved by falling rolls was returned to the education budget, there was no guarantee that it would be spent on special educational needs.

The teachers' unions were adamant that implementing the Act must mean extra resources for meeting special educational needs and that these resources should not be found from cutting back on other areas of provision. The National Association of Head Teachers, in response to the Dalebridge proposals for the implementation of the Education Act 1981 – proposals which contained plans to end the remedial service and establish an Assessment and Learning Support Service – stated that:

> While accepting that the implementation of the Act should be seen as a long-term process, we are convinced that local provision must be of sufficiently high quality as to ensure complete credibility. Adequate resources must be available as required so that the educational needs of *all pupils* can be met without any adverse effect . . . The financial allocation (£25,000) is *inadequate*. Resources must be available to provide even in its infancy an effective service with complete credibility. (Letter from Dalebridge NAHT to CEO, 17 May 1983.)

The National Association of Head Teachers had, of course, only to respond to the plans presented to it, as it did not have the responsibility for drawing up the plans. The proposed changes were not opposed, but it was stated that more resources would be needed. However, the ways in which the proposed allocations were inadequate were not spelled out, and no indication was made as to the additional resources considered to be necessary.

The position taken by the chief education officer, who had responsibility for implementing the Act, was quite different. In the document 'Proposals for the Implementation of the 1981 Education Act' presented to the schools sub-committee on 12th April 1983, he wrote:

> It will be the availability and quality of resources which determine the speed of progress. In spite of what has often been claimed in parliament and in DES press notices, the resource implications of the Act are enormous. While it is regrettable that no additional resources have been made available to local authorities, this in itself is not a reason for failing to adopt a positive approach.

While he considered that it would be highly desirable to have additional resources, he was charged with implementing the Act and providing as good a service as possible with the resources available.

A new adviser for special educational needs

In common with many LEAs, Dalebridge felt that a first priority for the future development of provision was the appointment of an adviser for special educational needs, and approval from the Education Committee was obtained in October 1983. This was the first in a series of new appointments and established a pattern of creating genuinely new positions and appointing people from outside the authority, using funds from internal reorganization rather than through increases in the budget.

The resignation of the chief adviser presented an opportunity to restructure the advisory service and to create new posts. Simultaneously with the resignation of the chief adviser, there was some debate about the structure of the authority's administration and the number of tiers that was appropriate for the efficient, smooth running of a small metropolitan authority. It was decided that the deputy chief education officer should take on the role of chief adviser in addition to his other duties. He was to have overall responsibility for the advisory service 'at a macro level' and the two existing senior advisers (4–11 years and 11–19 years) 'at a micro level' (Minutes, Schools Subcommittee, 11th October 1982). A major consideration in doing this was to secure a more effective integration of the administration and the advisory service. The salary saved by the resignation of the chief adviser was sufficient not only to appoint a general adviser for children with special educational needs but also to help – to the tune of £2,650 – finance another new post. Even though it was inadequate to cover the total cost, it provided an opportunity to present the elected members with a plan for a new appointment in multicultural education – an area that was of local concern.

The establishment of the Assessment and Learning Support Service

Central to the implementation of the Act, and the making of new provision for children with special educational needs in Dalebridge, was the creation of a new style of support service closely in line with the type of service recommended in the Warnock Report. This service, entitled the Assessment and Learning Support Service (ALSS), replaced the remedial reading service. Like most authorities, Dalebridge had operated a remedial reading service offering direct teaching help in small withdrawal groups to primary age children with reading problems. In the light of the new definitions of special need introduced by

Warnock, this service was seen to be too narrow in scope in relation to the age of the pupils helped, the type of special need provided for and the method of service delivery. It was envisaged that the new service would be concerned with children of all ages, although there would still be some concentration on younger children because it was hoped that the important initial assessment of special need would be made as early as possible. Also, while the secondary schools were large enough to operate their own special needs department, the primary schools – whose needs were more urgent – had traditionally been more dependent on help from outside, and this pattern was to continue.

The previous focus on remedial reading was perceived as being much too narrow. The new ALSS was to deal with the whole range of learning difficulties, including those caused by sensory impairment and physical handicap. In a paper presented to the school sub-committee on the 8th June 1983, the chief education officer also criticized the term 'remedial' and found it not only inadequate but positively misleading, when applied to the work he envisaged being undertaken by the ALSS. He quoted the following extract from Chapter 3 of the Warnock Report:

> The term 'remedial' . . . suggests that these children have something wrong with them that can be put right. It is true that some of them are suffering only a temporary learning difficulty and, given appropriate help, are able to return rapidly to their previous classes . . . Others, however, require special help and support throughout their school lives (3:39).

He went on to emphasize that where pupils needed extra help on a long-term basis the requisite provision had to be sustained. Moreover, if support had to be given on a long-term basis, it would be better provided from within the school. This constituted a further basis for the distinction between a remedial service concentrating exclusively on teaching withdrawal groups and the quite different role of the ALSS. The purpose of the latter would be to help children with special needs by working collaboratively with and through, rather than in place of, the class teacher: its prime roles would be assessment, advice, support and in-service training. The intention was clearly to make the new service quite distinct from the old; it would incorporate the work of the old but have significant new areas of concern and a new way of working.

Having received approval in principle from the elected members for the establishment of the new service, the administration had to achieve the necessary changes at the smallest extra cost. One solution would have been to create the new service in addition to the old, perhaps incorporating one into the other. This method had, in fact, been adopted by some authorities where, despite the prevailing economic gloom, there had still been real and significant growth in the budget. In Dalebridge, this sort of expansion was not a realistic option. Nevertheless, the elected members were persuaded that the creation of the new service was so highly desirable for improving the general standard of educational provision in the authority, and more directly for enabling Dalebridge to undertake its statutory obligations under the Act, that £25,000 was allocated in the 1983/84 budget for the creation of the service. This was the only new money made available for this major innovation, which was principally achieved by the redeployment and reallocation of existing teaching resources.

In essence, the new service was set up by capitalizing on the closure of the remedial service, the reading centre and a short-stay assessment centre, and the disestablishment of teaching posts within the school psychological service. By these actions, over 20 teaching posts became 'subject to change' and could be used for the establishment of the ALSS. The opportunity was taken to obtain approval for the introduction of two new key posts in April 1983, when the scheme was first put to the schools sub-committee. At this time there were resignations in two of the sectors adversely affected by the changes – the school psychological service and the short-stay assessment centre. It was essential that the head of the ALSS be appointed as soon as possible, and the opportunity to create this senior post came with the resignation of one of the educational psychologists. Instead of seeking a direct replacement, the chief education officer recommended that the vacant post be deleted from the establishment of the school psychological service, and the salary made available for the new post of head of the support service. At the same time a member of staff from the assessment centre left the authority, and this post was transferred to the ALSS for the creation of a specialist post of teacher for visually impaired children.

Like many authorities, Dalebridge considered it essential to appoint a specialist teacher for the visually impaired, in order for it to meet the requirements of the 1981 Act. Sections 5 and 7 of the Act, in detailing procedures for making assessments and Statements, required that, in the case of particular disabilities, the advice of a specialist teacher should be sought. Although it might be possible to use the services of such a teacher from a neighbouring authority, there were advantages to be gained from making a new appointment. In addition to contributing to assessments, the specialist teacher could help reduce the number of instances of extra-district placements for pupils with visual impairments. This would be both financially beneficial and in keeping with the authority's declared policy of keeping children in their local schools and communities wherever possible.

The total establishment of new posts in the ALSS was designed to create a team of staff with qualifications and experience covering the whole range of special needs in both segregated and mainstream settings. The new staff needed the professional and personal qualities to enable them to assess the needs of both pupils and teachers; to help teachers provide for all their pupils' needs; to allocate and supervise the work of non-teaching assistants; and to direct part-time teaching help. It was clear that these posts were quite different from those in the remedial service. On the closure of the remedial service, the reading centre and the assessment centre, the staff involved were offered redeployment with their salaries protected or early retirement if appropriate. They were invited to apply for any of the new posts, but they were given no special advantages. In fact, only four of the original employees entered the new service, and none of these were in the more senior positions.

The school psychological service

In common with most authorities, Dalebridge also achieved some expansion in the school psychological service. After a period of some uncertainty about the function and staffing of this service, which began with the school psychological service losing a post to the ALSS, and was followed over the next two years by a complete change of staff, the service ended up with five psychologists, as opposed to the four they had in 1978, with plans for a further additional post. This growth was achieved with no additional revenue, in fact, with a small temporary saving, as the newly appointed educational psychologists were all initially paid at points appreciably lower down the salary scales than their predecessors.

The establishment of a service for hearing impaired children

Unlike some of the changes in this authority, which were brought about with remarkable speed, the pace of change here was much slower. Traditionally, Dalebridge had made no provision of its own for hearing impaired children, but used the services of a neighbouring authority. In August 1980, a report produced by Dalebridge Special Education Working Party recommended that the authority should make its own provision. As a result the Dalebridge hearing impaired service was established in 1982, with a staff of two full-time teachers and ten full-time equivalent non-teaching assistants.

Significantly, thereafter, the number of hearing impaired children regarded as needing some form of special provision increased substantially. A survey conducted by the special education working party in 1980 had identified 84 pupils within Dalebridge who were defined as having hearing problems of varying degrees of severity; by October 1983 the number identified was 177, and by June 1985 this number had risen to 280. In the same month the chief education officer and assistant education officer for special needs submitted a paper to the education committee 'to demonstrate how the authority could seek to meet the needs of hearing impaired children within a Dalebridge mainstream setting, as an alternative to incurring equivalent or greater costs in extra-district charges by requiring the children to attend schools outside the authority' (paper presented to the Education Committee 10th June 1985).

Like many other authorities, Dalebridge saw opportunities for achieving both economies and change by reducing the number of their children placed in special schools outside the authority. Such placements were very expensive, generally involving either boarding provision or substantial travelling costs. So the desire to economize reinforced the principle of maximum integration and normalization in encouraging authorities to provide for more children in local schools.

The following passage is an extract from a paper presented by officers to the Dalebridge Education Committee in June 1985. After outlining the needs of the hearing impaired child and the work of the hearing impaired service, the paper goes on to specify the current situation, highlight its deficiencies and put forward a constructive plan, detailing the financial implications for remedying the present, unsatisfactory level of provision:

> *4. The Present Position*
>
> 4.1 The present staffing establishment of one qualified Teacher of the Deaf and one temporary ALSS Teacher (until July 1985) is chronically inadequate to deal with the number and nature of referrals and, as a result, the Authority cannot provide the necessary level of support required to be identified within statements under the 1981 Education Act.
>
> 4.2 The consequences of the present staffing position are:
>
> (a) In general terms 144 partially hearing children require an annual visit, a further 76 should be seen either monthly or at least four times per year. The majority are not receiving this frequency of visits. Five children who ought to be receiving significant amounts of direct teaching do not receive this provision, a further three

ceased to be provided with this facility in December 1984 but still need direct teaching.

(b) Our profoundly deaf/severely deaf children demand significant levels of time input. As the Authority is no longer able to support both the increasing numbers of partially hearing children in our schools *and* the profoundly deaf it is necessary that seven profoundly/severely deaf children are currently being 'statemented' according to the requirements of the 1981 Education Act. Clearly we cannot ignore the large number of partially hearing children completely. The only way that the profoundly/severely deaf can receive the levels of support necessary is to either
   (i) place the children in special schools outside the Authority at an average cost per pupil in 1985/6 of £6,500 in fees and £1,000 in transport (a total of £51,120); or
   (ii) increase the staffing levels of our own Hearing Impaired Service.

5. Financial Implications

In order to provide the minimal level of support necessary to meet the needs of the hearing impaired pupils identified above the following would be required:

	Assuming effective date January 1986:	*Financial year 1985/86* £	*Full year* £
1.	Regrading of present Head of Services post (Scale 3(S) to Scale 4)	110	430
2.	Regrading of present Support Teacher post (Scale 2(S) to Scale 3)	190	750
3.	Support Teachers 2 x Scale 3 plus NI/Superannuation	5,370	21,460
4.	Non Teaching Assistance 150 hours per week x 38 weeks	4,620	18,470
5.	Equipment	2,000	2,000
6.	Travelling expenses	380	1,500
7.	Secretarial assistance 10 hours per week x 38 weeks	300	1,190
	Total	12,970	45,800

	Financial year 1985/86 £	*Full year* £
The alternative would be: cost of day school provision in extra district special schools (from September 1985)		
Extra district charges £6,500 p.a. x 7	26,540	45,500
Travel £5 per day x 190 x 7	3,880	6,650
Total	30,420	52,150

There is sufficient budget provision for the extra district charges in 1985/86 but a shortfall of £15,500 in future years, but this will probably become available as other children leave their present extra district schools.

Under normal circumstances the Council's budget procedures would allow this budget provision to be offered as compensatory savings to fund the increased costs of the Authority's provision for the Hearing Impaired Service.

However, recent changes in the Council's financial regulations mean that until this committee's projected over-spending of £239,160 have been eradicated, virement must be approved by finance sub committee. The request to finance sub committee must include the special circumstances for the request. The special circumstances in this case are that the savings will not arise without the implementation of the proposals for the Hearing Impaired Service.

Approval of Policy and Resources Committee is also required because the proposals involve a major change in the level of service.

6. *Recommendations*

It is recommended:

(a) That the revised establishment of the Hearing Impaired Service outlined in (5) above be approved in view of:

(i) Approval would be in line with the philosophical basis already accepted by the Authority that, in accordance with the recommendations of the Warnock Report and the spirit of the 1981 Education Act, special educational needs should be met in a mainstream setting wherever this is practicable.

(ii) The Service is already established with parents and schools as an effective service, meeting the needs of the pupils that it is presently able to deal with. A number of letters of support for the service have been received from parents of hearing impaired children strongly preferring placement in a mainstream school to placement in a special school outside the Authority.

(iii) Expansion of the Hearing Impaired Service is cost effective in terms of the overall budget. Since the service was first established substantial savings have been made in the extra district budgets of 1983/4 and 1984/5 which more than met the cost of establishing the service.

(iv) Resources are spent developing the Authority's own service over which it has control rather than spending 'dead' money in another Authority. Expertise is built up within the Authority's own specialist and mainstream staff that can be applied to future children. A degree of flexibility is available to meet any changing patterns of demand within the Authority.

(b) That Finance Sub Committee be requested to approve virement of £12,970 in 1985/6 and £45,800 in future years from extra district charges.

(c) That Personnel Sub Committee be requested to approve the additional non-teaching and secretarial assistance.

31.5.85

There are several particular points of interest in this approach. First, the children being considered were not at the time in extra-district placements; it was future provision for these children that was being discussed. This is in line with the policy and practice of other authorities. Although there are individual examples of children who, for a variety of reasons, have been moved from extra-district schools, more usually the debate revolves around future placements of children. So it is potential savings from future budgets that are being debated, not actual savings from current budgets. Nevertheless, children who may be considered for extra-district placement are virtually always children who have acute needs, and although these needs may certainly be met in an ordinary school within the authority, they undoubtedly require the provision of extra specialist support. Stopping extra-district placements and simply placing the children unsupported in ordinary schools is not a realistic option. Therefore, it is fair to compare the relative costs of extra-district placement with placement plus support in ordinary schools.

As can be seen by looking at the financial implications presented in the paper, the restructuring and expansion of the hearing impaired service is, in fact, cheaper than extra-district placements for seven children. These particular children would be in day school provision, but with additional transport costs. Had the option been residential schools, which a great many LEAs use for extra-district placements, then the potential savings made by providing within the authority would have been even greater. Alternatively, more resources could have been made available for meeting special needs in ordinary schools.

Secondly, the proposals illustrate the direct and tight control exercised by the elected members. It used to be the case that money could be moved with relative ease from one budget heading to another, but in recent years all virement in this authority has had to be approved by the finance sub-committee. At the time of the report, the education committee was operating a deficit budget and one of the methods used to deal with this situation was to regard savings made under one budget heading as money to be set against the deficit, not as money that could be made available for other uses within the education service. If any virement was to take place, it had to be explicitly approved, but, of course, virement was still the only obvious way to accomplish change through local initiatives within the existing budgetary framework at a time when there was no overall growth in the system.

The particular case presented in support of the changes in the hearing impaired service revolved around the fact that the proposed improvements themselves would result in savings. Special provision had to be made for the children involved – it was not optional. This being the case, the changes suggested, it was argued, would result in a type of provision that was both superior to and cheaper than the alternative. It was an unusual circumstance to find that both educational interests and financial economy led to the same conclusion. The expansion of the hearing impaired service would also enable expertise to be built up within the authority's own specialist and mainstream staff. In the future, pupils with all levels of hearing impairment would have their special needs met in the authority's ordinary schools. This would include pupils with severe hearing loss who were at present in special schools and also pupils with milder or temporary problems who were in ordinary schools but not currently receiving any special help. In contrast, money used for extra-district placements was regarded as 'dead' money handed over to another authority with consequent loss of control.

The establishment of provision for children with speech impairments

Similar arguments were also successfully used for new provision within the authority for children with speech and language impairments. For younger pupils there was already an established special language unit attached to a primary school, but there was no specialist provision for pupils of secondary school age. Pupils leaving the primary unit either went unsupported into a secondary school or to specialist residential provision in a neighbouring authority. The opportunity for a change in provision occurred when the future schooling of two children leaving the primary unit in the summer of 1984 was considered. Here, in addition to the arguments put forward in the case of the hearing impaired service, parental rights under the Act were also used. In a paper presented to the Education Committee in April 1984 the chief education officer put the position very clearly:

> The issue facing the authority from August might appear to be a straightforward one of deciding how to resource the future education of two children. However, in both cases the parents are unlikely to support residential provision and if the cases were to go to final appeal it is probable that the Secretary of State would not support the authority. The present position is therefore as much about parental aspirations and the new legal framework as it is about resources. However, given the inevitability of having to incur expenditure, the present position also presents an opportunity.

Here the administrator accepted the realities of the situation and, instead of being constrained by them, used them as a platform from which to launch innovations that would in fact be seen as desirable even without the legal and financial constraints. The cost of schooling and travel for two children for a five-day residential placement in the school year 1985/86 would total £25,000 in a full year, whereas for rather less than that sum a network of local provision could be developed, which would not only incur less expenditure in the short term but produce even greater long-term savings, keep children within their own communities and families, and contribute significantly to the achievement of the authority's policy of meeting special educational needs in the mainstream wherever practicable.

4 The Matrix of Provision

There are a great many ways in which the extra provision required by pupils with special needs in ordinary schools can be supplied. They include the establishment of designated special needs posts, special units attached to ordinary schools, help provided through links established between special and ordinary schools, and the work of a wide range of local authority support services.

The complex issue of the nature of the 'extra' provision has already been discussed. Equally contentious is the question of the number of pupils who are to be regarded as having special needs and the proportion of them who will actually receive extra help. Pupils who are the subjects of Statements have their 'extra' provision legally guaranteed under the 1981 Act, but even in authorities which have a high level of Statementing they will still be a very small proportion of the total number of pupils who have special needs. Many of these other pupils will have to rely on their classroom teachers to cater for their needs. A proportion of them will receive some form of additional help, usually through one of the support services, that will come within the 'provision generally made by the authority'. The number of pupils directly helped by the support services varies enormously between authorities, but nowhere does it approach the 20 per cent of pupils estimated by Warnock to have special needs at some stage of their school careers.

How to allocate extra resources to schools

Let us consider one pupil who is identified as needing help over and above that which is currently available in the ordinary classroom, and who is going to remain in the ordinary school. How can additional help be offered and, in outline, what form can it take? First, a distinction can be made between help offered directly to the pupil and help that is given to the teacher from which it is hoped that the pupil will benefit. Secondly, a distinction can be drawn between the provision of expert help and advice, and assistance of a less specialized kind. Useful distinctions can also be made between support provided from resources controlled by the school rather than the authority, and those used inside, as opposed to outside the school.

(a) *Help direct to the pupil*

1) The pupil can receive constant individual teaching or other assistance in or out of the classroom provided by an additional teacher or non-teaching assistant.
2) Provision may be made in a special unit or class in the ordinary school with a small group of other pupils.
3) Provision may involve a combination of 1) and 2) with pupils spending part of their time in the unit and part in the ordinary classroom (often supported by a teacher or ancillary).
4) The pupil may spend most of his or her time in the classroom, but receive regular extra help either in the classroom or through withdrawal for individual or small group attention.
5) The pupil may be in the ordinary classroom but engaged in a special programme of work prepared and supervised by a support service and administered by the class teacher.

This last method of direct help to the pupil merges with category (b).

(b) *Indirect help* where the assistance is given to the teacher rather than the child.

1) Advice on catering for the special needs of a particular pupil may be provided by the school psychological service or one of the other support services.
2) Instead of the advice being directed specifically to the needs of one particular pupil, it may be directed to the solving of particular types of problems and adopting particular strategies for coping.

All support that takes the form of advice given to practising teachers can be regarded as a type of in-service training, particularly, of course, when it is concerned with more general matters.

Help given to pupils and teachers may be 'expert', involving specialist knowledge and skills, or it may take the form of giving assistance which, while being valuable, does not go beyond the competence of the classroom teacher. From our research, it seems very important that the nature of the support that class teachers can expect is made explicit; this is particularly so when the help is provided from outside the school, usually by a support service. If the support service is offering expert help and advice, the basis of the expertise needs to be made clear. This is unlikely to be a problem in the case of services for the sensory impaired, for example, where the support staff have specialist qualifications and experience of teaching pupils with a particular disability. In such circumstances, classroom teachers and the support service staff are unlikely to experience any serious disagreement over their respective roles.

A different situation prevails for support services operating in the areas of learning difficulties and behaviour problems, and they need to negotiate carefully on the exact nature of the support they have to offer. If the help being offered is basically 'another pair of hands in the classroom', both the teacher and the support staff must know who directs the work of the support staff and what they can be expected to do. On the other hand, if the support is intended to take the form of expert help and advice it must live up to the reasonable expectations of the class teacher. Most teachers have experience of teaching pupils with mild learning difficulties and pupils with behaviour problems. Many of them feel confident in their ability to provide for these pupils – if they had smaller classes and more time to give individual attention (Gipps and Gross, 1986). Teachers in this position may still need and want expert help and advice, but the credibility of the advice and those giving it must be clearly established. One of the major developments currently under way (and discussed in detail in Chapter 6) is the transformation of peripatetic remedial services into 'special educational needs advisory and support services'. The role of the peripatetic remedial teacher is quite different from that of the advisory teacher, and it is essential to the successful operation of the new service that more than a change of job title occurs.

All of the forms of provision mentioned can be supplied in a variety of ways:

1) extra resources in the form of staff, equipment and materials put into a school for use at the head's discretion – an arrangement very similar to the EPA arrangements;
2) extra resources based in and part of the school, but specifically directed to provision for pupils with special needs;
3) resources based and controlled outside the school, usually going into the school but sometimes involving teachers and pupils coming out;
4) no extra resources in the form of staff or equipment but efforts directed towards the improvement and more effective use of resources that are already there. The main example

here is in-service training, but initiatives such as utilizing accommodation newly available because of falling rolls also belong here.

These different ways of providing support can be represented as a matrix of provision, as in Table 4.1. The boxes are filled in by examples of the type of provision that can be made within the various frameworks; they are only examples and it must be remembered that they do not represent the only type of provision that can be made.

Table 4.1: *Matrix of provision*

	Extra resources to school as a whole (EPA type)	*Extra resources to school specifically for special needs*	*Externally controlled resources used in the school*	*Externally controlled resources used out of school*
Direct to pupil	Non-teaching assistant attached to pupil	Special needs teacher taking small withdrawal groups	Special Educational Needs Support and Advisory Service teacher working with pupils	Off-site units progress centres
Indirect	Better staff/ pupil ratio	Special units (staff offering advice to other teachers)	Special Educational Needs Support and Advisory Service offering advice to other teachers	INSET courses

1. Extra resources, based on an assessment of the special needs present in a school, can be allocated to the school and the detailed provision decided internally. The extra resources may take the form of direct help to individual children or be used indirectly, for instance to achieve a generally more favourable pupil–teacher ratio.

2. Extra resources may be allocated to schools but 'earmarked' for specific purposes. This type of arrangement may take the form of a teacher or an ancillary helper assigned specifically to one pupil. If this form of organization of resources is used for indirect rather than direct help, it may involve maintaining a special needs unit, which in addition to its own teaching commitment offers advice and support to mainstream staff.

3. Externally controlled and directed resources which are used in the school usually come from the support services which include the school psychological service, special education needs advisory and support service and services for the visually and hearing impaired. All these services can work either directly with pupils or indirectly through teachers.

4. Extra resources can also be both controlled and used out of the school, for instance in the provision of off-site units and progress centres where help is given directly to the pupils. Where this type of organization of resources is used to provide indirect support, the most likely form is INSET courses usually run by higher education institutions. It can be argued that this type of indirect provision must not be regarded as providing extra support as far as individual pupils are concerned. Any additional expertise that the class or subject teacher acquires during in-service training will improve the general level of provision and may result in 'extra' provision being unnecessary, but cannot itself be regarded as constituting 'extra to what is generally available in schools in the authority'. Nevertheless, the resources needed to run courses are significant and, depending on the exact method of financing, this type of provision may be in direct competition for funds with other methods of providing for special educational needs.

Each one of the ways of allocating resources will now be considered. It should be remembered that no one method precludes an authority from using the others and that any individual organization or even person may be involved in more than one system of delivery.

Resources given to the school as a whole

To some extent ordinary schools have always been called upon to provide for pupils with special needs from their own resources. The estimated 18 per cent of pupils with special needs have always been educated in ordinary schools, and many of the pupils who eventually went to special schools first, had their needs recognized while in ordinary schools. Although it is impossible to say how many pupils were involved, there were without doubt pupils with severe and complex special needs being educated in ordinary schools before the 1981 Act gave them the protection of a Statement.

Much of the special needs work undertaken in primary schools was undertaken by part-time staff who were used for remedial work at the discretion of the head. Economies of recent years have seen a reduction in the number of part-time staff, and this in turn has resulted in less provision for children with special needs at a time when there was increasing concern over this aspect of education (Croll and Moses, 1985). At the time of the implementation of the 1981 Act, primary heads were very worried about the decrease in the availability of part-time staff and the effect this was having on the remedial work of their schools.

When pupil–teacher ratios are relatively generous it is possible for primary headteachers to allocate staff specifically to special needs work. However, in recent years many primary schools have had staffing levels that require all staff except the head to be in charge of a class. Falling rolls may mean that the overall pupil–teacher ratio in a school still *seems* quite favourable, but grouping the pupils appropriately into classes may still require the whole staff. When this happens the only 'extra' provision of any sort must come either from the head or from other members of staff, while the head acts as class teacher. Inevitably, the many commitments of primary headteachers mean that such activities cannot be either extensive or regular.

Additional complications are created when classes have to be covered for absent staff. Even where there is an extra teacher without regular class duties who could do special needs work, covering classes may be given precedence over providing special needs assistance, a situation which applies equally in secondary schools. The problems created by falling rolls are similar, though not identical. Again, while the overall pupil–teacher ratio may appear favourable, there may well be staff shortages in some areas of the curriculum. Curriculum-led staffing policies do seek to overcome this problem, but at a time of economic stringency complete implementation is likely to be difficult, if not impossible.

Schools of all kinds also face acute problems of competing priorities. There are many areas to be provided for, and a whole range of initiatives that schools are being asked to undertake. Even in schools where catering for special needs is considered to be of great importance, activities like the introduction of microcomputers, establishing links with industry, introducing GCSE, developing new approaches to the teaching of maths and so on, may take precedence or at least be in competition for the funds available. It can, of course, be argued that any new initiative in, say, the teaching of mathematics should include an element specializing in mathematics for slow learners and pupils with other special needs, and that, if all curriculum innovations had a special needs element integrated into them, specialist special needs activities could become superfluous. This might perhaps be a desirable long-term aim, but it is at least equally arguable that in present circumstances it is the separateness of special needs provision that ensures its continued existence and expansion.

Schools may receive extra resources for special educational needs in a variety of ways. The proportion of children with special needs in different schools varies enormously. Virtually no school will be without some children who have special needs, but many will have in excess of 50 per cent. Obviously, therefore, some schools will have to allocate a higher proportion of their total resources to special needs activities than others. Where no direction is given about the internal allocation of resources, the decision is in the hands of the headteacher, who has to balance the various conflicting demands.

This does not apply to children with Statements (at least it is the intention of the legislation that it should not). The Statement should guarantee that, wherever necessary, a pupil will receive provision that is extra to what is generally available in the ordinary schools in an authority. It is for this reason that when the Act was first implemented many headteachers were anxious to get Statements written for as many children as possible, in the belief that it was a way of acquiring additional resources. However, in some cases Statements were actually written requiring a school to find the 'extra' provision for a given pupil – usually in the form of individual or small group teaching time – from within its own resources!

Specifically allocated resources

It has long been recognized that school policy and practice should take account of the great variation between the catchment areas of schools, and the home and cultural background of pupils. The Educational Priority Area scheme was based on the recognition of these differences, and similar policies are still operated by many local authorities. With the growing interest in and awareness of special needs, it is increasingly widespread practice to include a special needs component in systems for allocating additional resources to schools, over and above the indices relating to ethnicity, poverty and deprivation (which may themselves be related to special needs). This can take a variety of forms, but is usually based primarily, if not exclusively, on the results of standardized tests of achievement, particularly of reading. In their study of LEA screening procedures, Gipps *et al.* (1983) found that one of the principal reasons that LEAs gave for operating testing programmes was to identify children who had difficulties which required additional help, and therefore differential allocation of resources.

The 'differential resources' are usually in the form of extra teacher hours, which can be supplied in a variety of ways. Under an Education Priority Area type system, this can take the form of additional full- or part-time staff appointed to the school, to be used at the discretion of the head, either directly for special needs work or in a more general capacity. The head can decide to use these extra hours in a variety of ways: to offer help to individual children either in the classroom or withdrawn from it; to establish a post of special needs 'enabler'; to expand in an area of the curriculum not directly related to special needs that the school would like to offer its pupils; or to enable class sizes to be reduced. A reduction in class sizes is what primary teachers would most like to see and what they believe would be most advantageous in helping them to provide for pupils with special educational needs (Gipps *et al.*, 1986). However, it is unusual for authorities to allow headteachers complete freedom in this way, but there are a number of pilot schemes in operation which are exploring the viability of giving headteachers much closer control over their school budgets and the associated decision-making than has previously been common practice. In such circumstances, as already indicated, there may be considerable pressure from within the school to divert extra help away from special needs. It must also be remembered that the authority remains directly responsible for the extra educational provision required by any pupils who have Statements and cannot properly discharge their duty under the Act by handing over responsibility entirely to the school.

A more usual arrangement is for the authority to allocate to schools extra resources 'earmarked' for particular purposes and in particular ways. The administration of these resources may be in the hands of the headteacher, who is likely to have some leeway to exercise discretion, but the direction of the funding is decided in the Education Office. The exact form that this type of arrangement can take is again quite varied; two that are widespread will be considered here: the operation of a system of designated special needs posts; and the establishment and running of a special unit attached to an ordinary school.

Designated posts

Many authorities operate a system of designated special needs posts in schools. Schools that are considered to need additional provision in order to cater properly for their pupils with special needs are allocated an additional post on top of the normal staffing establishment, on the explicit understanding that the teacher appointed to the post will be concerned exclusively with special needs. This is an arrangement more frequently used for secondary than for primary schools: additional help for primary schools is more likely to be in the form of assistance from the support services.

As previously mentioned, schools are usually allocated a designated special needs post on the basis of an index of need. Such appointments are usually negotiated with the headteacher, and most designated special needs teachers start off with a remit that has been agreed by all parties concerned. The original job description may well be produced within the Education Office but will normally be subject to modification. Once appointed to such a post, the teacher becomes responsible to the head of the school, where developments in provision can force changes in priorities. It is possible, for instance, that the number of pupils with special needs in a school decreases because of a generally declining school roll or a change in the nature of the catchment area, or it may be that the designated teacher has been particularly successful in enabling class or subject teachers to make better provision for their pupils who have special needs. In these circumstances, both schools and local authorities may feel the need for greater flexibility of staffing than is possible under a system of designated posts. A response to this problem can be for holders of designated posts not to be appointed to an individual school and responsible to its headteacher, but to be part of a support service controlled and run outside the school. This system is increasingly favoured by authorities and is described in detail in Chapter 6.

The strength of the designated post system is that it enables schools themselves to cater for the vast majority of their pupils with special needs. (Additional support may still be needed for pupils with severe and/or unusual needs.) Continually having to call for outside assistance may encourage teachers to feel that special needs are not primarily their responsibility. On the other hand, when there is an overall shortage of special education expertise, careful deployment of existing skills is of great importance.

One way of striking a balance between ensuring that schools have some internal special needs skills and deploying the available specialist expertise to best effect, is to combine a support service external to the school with a scheme for each school to have a member of staff with specific responsibility for special needs. This idea was first put forward in the Warnock Report and many authorities have since established the practice. Teachers who become their school's special needs 'co-ordinator' or 'enabler' (a variety of titles are given to the holders of these posts) are not normally new appointments – they are drawn from the existing staff of the school and do not necessarily have all the knowledge and skills required. Training teachers to take on this role has become a major thrust of in-service training in special needs (see the companion volume on INSET for special educational needs (Hegarty and Moses, 1988)).

The special unit

A special unit attached to an ordinary school is a long-established form of provision for pupils with special educational needs. A wide range of special needs can be catered for in this type of provision. (There are units, particularly for pupils with behaviour or discipline problems, which are not attached to particular schools.) Pupils in special units are usually the subject of Statements, and this provision tends to be regarded as part of the 'special sector' of education.

The extent to which a special unit attached to an ordinary school can be considered part of that school varies a great deal, and in individual instances can be difficult to assess. It is possible for a unit to be geographically located at a school but for it to have virtually no contact with the main body of the school. However, the intention of unit provision is to facilitate the integration of pupils with special educational needs, and Hegarty and Pocklington (1982) have documented the successful integration of pupils from units. In some circumstances, individual pupils can be integrated from a unit into the ordinary school without extra support for the ordinary school. This can happen if pupils registered in the unit attend mainstream classes on a full-time basis and the staff of the unit are totally engaged with pupils who spend most of their time in the unit. In such instances, individual pupils may well be successfully integrated into the mainstream but the unit cannot be said to be offering support to the ordinary school. Indeed, if the concept of support is used in this context, it might be more accurate to say that the school is supporting the unit.

There are many ways in which the main school, both staff and pupils, can be supported by a unit. The unit is likely to specialize in offering provision to pupils with a particular type of special need, usually of a severe or complex nature. The example of unit provision for the hearing impaired provides an illustration. Most usually, the unit will be established to cater for pupils who have severe hearing impairments and are assessed as requiring special provision normally based on the use of hearing aids and specialized teaching techniques. The nature of the impairment may require that these services are received in a special unit rather than in the regular classroom, though it should be remembered that there are several accounts of the successful integration into ordinary classrooms of pupils of all ages with severe hearing impairments (Lynas, 1986).

One of the factors that can greatly affect the integration process is the support given by the specialist staff of the unit to classroom teachers. This can take the form of training courses run for staff, more informal advice, and the passing on of information and support by the unit teacher actually in the classroom. Also, when classroom teachers have gained some experience of teaching pupils with hearing impairments in their classes, the mere presence on site of specialist staff who can be called upon if problems do occur will encourage class teachers to cater for hearing impaired pupils. Although some pupils may require unit provision because of their hearing impairments, many others have some sort of hearing difficulty, even if it is only of a temporary nature. The experience of teaching pupils with serious difficulties, particularly with the support of specialist staff, can make class teachers more aware of hearing problems, enhance their understanding of them and enable them to cope better with pupils who have hearing problems.

In addition to the support offered by the teaching staff of a unit, the school may also benefit from the unit's ancillary staff. While the smooth running of the unit is likely to require most of the help available, there are instances where a proportion of the ancillary assistants' time can be deployed in the main school to the mutual benefit of school and unit.

Although close collaboration between main school and unit is likely to be facilitated by the unit being organizationally part of the school, this is by no means universal. It is common practice for the head of a unit to work to either an education officer or an adviser with responsibility for special educational needs. This is particularly common where the head of the unit is also head of a peripatetic support service. The combination of running a special unit and a peripatetic service, in addition to being directly responsible to the Education Office, all tend to distance the activities of a unit from the school. However, it is still possible for close working relationships to be established and maintained, although much depends upon the individual attitudes and initiatives of the staff involved. Even where the unit staff are ultimately accountable to an education officer or adviser, there is always the understanding that in the day-to-day operation of the unit they are in some measure responsible to the head of the school, though their position is clearly different from that of teachers on the school establishment. In these circumstances the nature of the relationship between school and unit will have to be carefully negotiated, as the lines of responsibility are both complicated and tenuous.

Despite these potential hazards, this system of organization is favoured by many authorities. Its main advantages lie in the greater flexibility it offers and in the closer control that can be achieved. The number of children with a particular special need and their geographical distribution may change over a period of time, as may the type of provision thought appropriate for them. Specialist staff appointed directly to the education authority can be used more flexibly in response to such changes and, particularly if the special unit is also part of a peripatetic service, the range of provision offered to pupils can be wider and more directly suited to individual needs. The arrangement also ensures that specialist teaching staff are used solely for specialist work, not general teaching duties.

Externally controlled and directed services used in the school

Certain types of support are both controlled and directed from outside the school, the most widespread example being formally designated support services. The work of local authority support services is the subject of the following chapters and need not be considered further here. Another example of this form of support is provided by link arrangements between special and ordinary schools. This novel development, which is dealt with in detail in a companion volume (Jowett *et al.*, 1988), is briefly outlined below.

Links between special and ordinary schools

In addition to the expansion and reorganization of the various special needs support services and the development of school-based initiatives, a new type of initiative recommended in the Warnock Report which involves the establishment of links between special and ordinary schools is now becoming widespread. This innovation is particularly noteworthy as it involves unusual types of contact between what were previously, for the most part, separate sectors of the education system. Link schemes mark a significant departure in educational provision. They embody such unusual practices as teachers working in schools other than the one to which they were appointed and outside the jurisdiction of the headteacher to whom they are responsible; pupils attending two schools or attending one school while being on the roll of another; and resources acquired by one school being used principally in another.

Link schemes can take a great variety of forms and differ considerably in their significance. Some schemes represent only minor changes in practice and provision, whereas others can justifiably be regarded as major reforms, constituting real moves towards a more de-segregated and truly comprehensive education system. The more substantial links formed between special and ordinary schools may represent just as significant a form of integration as those involving the individual placement of children. They can enable the particular characteristics of special education to be more readily available to pupils in ordinary schools, while at the same time allowing those who really need special school placements to gain experience of ordinary schools.

It is at first sight surprising that link schemes, having so many innovative features, are now so very widespread. Jowett *et al.* (1988) report a survey conducted in 1985 covering all the special schools in 26 local authorities. Three-quarters of the schools were at that time involved in link arrangements, and a further one-tenth of them had plans for links in the near future. Two-thirds of the special schools had staff spending varying amounts of time in ordinary schools acting, in many ways, like a support service. When special school teachers went into ordinary schools, they were most likely to spend their time teaching combined groups of pupils from both schools, but they also taught groups comprised solely of special school pupils. A substantial amount of their time was also spent advising mainstream teachers. Most special school staff spent no more than a few hours each week in other schools, but a quarter of the teachers in the survey were working outside their own school for one or more days a week and in a few cases were spending the entire week working in other schools.

Some special school pupils also had very different experiences of school as a result of link schemes. Altogether 62 per cent of the special schools surveyed had pupils who spent varying amounts of the school week in ordinary schools, either individually or in groups. More than half of the pupils who attended ordinary schools on an individual basis did so for at least one day a week, and for many children this arrangement represented a major step along the road to full integration. For other pupils with severe and complex difficulties, who would continue to require a special school education, attending an ordinary school as a member of a group for a few hours each week still represented a significant move towards giving them valuable experiences that they would not otherwise have of life in ordinary schools.

Link schemes have been developed for a variety of reasons, pragmatic and philosophical, at both authority and school levels. Falling rolls have made some special schools fearful for their future, and have created situations for local authorities where difficult decisions have had to be taken over staffing levels and the viability of small special schools. Both individual schools and LEAs have grasped the opportunity presented by this situation to look for new roles for special schools and their staff. An option taken by many has been to maintain staffing levels in special schools, despite a reduction in the number of pupils, and to use the advantageous levels of staffing to establish link schemes with ordinary schools, thus retaining and using to maximum advantage the expertise of its special school teachers.

Some of the earliest link schemes were established by special schools which, besides fearing the consequences of falling rolls, felt seriously threatened by Warnock's proposals for integrating pupils with special needs into ordinary schools. But the special schools were not motivated only by fears about survival. There were a number of forward-looking headteachers who eagerly grasped the opportunity to show the rest of the educational world what they could do and make the expertise of the special school staff more widely available throughout the system.

A further motivation for link schemes is the belief that they offer unique opportunities for certain pupils to move into ordinary schools. Such schemes inevitably reduce the amount of teaching done in special schools; they also reduce the time pupils spend in special schools and are likely to reduce the actual numbers on roll. The general aim is to maximize the amount of time pupils spend in the mainstream, but to do so gradually and flexibly, using the link to provide a progressive series of steps leading ultimately to full-time, permanent placement in the ordinary school. One of the outstanding characteristics of many of the schemes is their dynamic nature. They will not, once established, necessarily continue in close approximation with their original form. During the course of the research, three schools were observed taking irreversible steps towards total absorption by the ordinary schools to which they were linked. The period of the link was seen as a time to ensure that the ordinary school and its teachers were adequately prepared and to establish appropriate continuing support for the pupils with special needs in the school.

Externally controlled resources used outside the school

Yet another type of provision is controlled, directed and provided outside the school. The principal example here is one of indirect provision, viz in-service training, whereby the schools' capacity to provide for pupils with special needs is enhanced. This is discussed in the companion volume by Hegarty and Moses (1988).

The most extreme example of this type of provision offered direct to pupils is the off-site unit which can be just as cut off from the ordinary school as the traditional special school and more isolated than many now are since the development of link schemes. This type of unit usually caters for pupils with behavioural or emotional problems and/or those who present the ordinary school with management problems. Although these units are by definition not attached to schools, they can also act as a base from which support services are run to help schools with behaviour and management problems. Where this is not the case and a unit caters solely for the pupils who attend, it can only be regarded as supporting the ordinary school in a very indirect sense by removing the pupils that the school finds impossible to manage or educate. It does not provide support in the sense of helping the school to overcome its difficulties and retain the pupils.

Other off-site provision may include reading centres and 'progress' centres. In most instances pupils do not attend full-time but are withdrawn from their regular classroom for a number of periods each week for specialist help at the centre. Usually, though not always, these off-site centres offer 'remedial' teaching in reading and language. There seems to be a move away from taking pupils out of school for this type of help and a correspondingly greater concentration on providing help within the school, either by the school's own staff or through the support services.

5 The Special Educational Needs Advisers

Number of advisers in post

Since 1978 there has been a substantial increase in the number of advisers for special educational needs appointed by the LEAs. In that year the Warnock Committee estimated that only about two-thirds of all authorities had a special educational adviser in post. More advisers were subsequently appointed, at least in part, as a result of Warnock's recommendations, but the increase accelerated in 1983 at the time of the implementation of the 1981 Act. By 1985, very nearly 90 per cent of the responding authorities had at least one adviser for special educational needs. It seems to have been the need to implement the legislation that acted as the main spur to the creation of the new posts. Although the requirements of the Act did not necessitate the appointment of advisers in the same way as they did educational psychologists, the appointment of an adviser was one of the most obvious ways in which the LEAs could demonstrate their concern about, and commitment to improving educational provision for, children with special educational needs.

Table 5.1: *Percentage of LEAs with various numbers of special educational needs advisers, 1985*

	Number of special educational needs advisers in post					
Types of LEA	*0*	*1*	*2*	*3*	*4*	*5+*
Shire counties *N*=36	5.5	50.0	25.0	14.0	5.5	0
Metropolitans *N*=25	20.0	64.0	8.0	8.0	0	0
London boroughs and ILEA *N*=16	6.25	75.0	12.5	0	0	6.25*
Total 77	10.4	59.7	16.9	9.1	2.6	1.3

* ILEA has 38 special educational needs advisers

Table 5.1 indicates the percentage of different types of LEA which employ varying numbers of special educational needs advisers. The most usual arrangement overall is for authorities to have one special needs adviser; 75 per cent of London boroughs and 64 per cent of metropolitan authorities have this level of staffing. No London borough employs more than two, and only eight per cent of metropolitan authorities employ three advisers for special educational needs. As would be expected the shire counties, being on the whole larger authorities, employ a greater number of advisers more frequently. Nevertheless, 50 per cent still have only one such post and no shire county has as many as five. It is perhaps worth remarking that whereas only two shire counties and one London borough had no adviser for special needs, no fewer than five metropolitan authorities (20 per cent) were without such a post.

These levels of staffing represent a considerable increase since 1978. Over 30 per cent of the responding authorities had created new posts; nearly 17 per cent of authorities which previously had no adviser now had one, and over 12 per cent of authorities had increased their advisory staff. These changes are detailed in Tables 5.2(a) and (b).

Table 5.2(a): *Percentage of LEAs with new special educational needs advisory posts*

	% LEAs
Shire counties *N*=36	25.00
Metropolitans *N*=25	24.00
London boroughs; and ILEA *N*=16	56.25
Total = 77	31.20

Table 5.2(b): *Percentage of LEAs appointing a special educational needs adviser (i) for the first time and (ii) as an additional post*

	First time	*Additional post*
Shire counties *N*=36	8.3	16.7
Metropolitans *N*=25	12.0	12.0
London boroughs and ILEA *N*=16	43.7	12.5
Total = 77	16.9	14.3

Changes were most apparent in the London boroughs, where over half the responding authorities had created new posts; in all but two instances a special educational needs adviser was appointed for the first time. Fewer metropolitan authorities created new posts and those that did were equally divided between those who were appointing a special needs adviser for the first time and those who were adding to their advisory staff. A quarter of the county authorities established new posts, mostly to add to existing special needs advisory staff. Nearly all the increases involved the creation of just one new post, but three county authorities appointed two new advisers.

Advisers for special educational needs can find themselves in a variety of different types of advisory service. Table 5.3 gives information on the size of advisory teams in general and the average number of special needs advisers per team.

Table 5.3: *The average number of all advisers and the average number of special educational needs advisers employed by LEAs*

LEA	*All advisers*	*Special needs advisers*
Shire counties *N*=36	23.0	1.6
Metropolitans *N*=25	15.5	1.2
London boroughs *N*=15 (excluding ILEA)	11.7	1.1

There is a considerable range in the size of advisory teams in the counties and the metropolitan boroughs. The London boroughs, excluding ILEA, are much more consistent. Six counties have 15 or fewer advisers, whereas four have advisory teams of 35 or over, the largest being over 50. There is also a considerable range in the metropolitan authorities, with three authorities having ten or fewer advisers and six having 20 or more, the largest having 38.

As previously indicated in Table 5.1, authorities are most likely to have one special needs adviser. This means that in the metropolitan authorities the special needs adviser is likely to be one in a team of about 15, and in the London boroughs, one in a team of about 12. In the county authorities there is still likely to be only one special needs adviser in a much larger team of advisers, but in some instances there are two or more. One shire county has 27 advisers but no one specifically responsible for special needs, and two counties have one adviser for special needs each in advisory teams of 33 and 34. By contrast, two county advisory teams of 14 and 16 respectively include four special needs advisers each.

Other significant changes have occurred in the level and type of special needs advisory staff provided by LEAs. In some instances when new appointments were made to previously established posts, the opportunity was taken to modify the nature of the job, broadening its scope from a near-exclusive concern with special schools and units, to a general involvement with provision in ordinary schools. In other instances, the job was redefined in similar ways while still being undertaken by the person already in post. The increased importance attached to the area of special needs is evident not only in the number of new posts created, but also in the upgrading of existing posts, adding to the status of staff involved in special needs work.

The role of the special educational needs adviser

The work undertaken by advisers is multi-faceted and difficult to define. Information collected from four advisers and one advisory headteacher visited during this research indicated the many demands made upon their time and the variety of activities subsumed under their job description. They were supporting other staff responsible for pupils with special needs and providing them with advice and information. Their work had a developmental element involving a commitment to in-service training and committee work. Administration formed another component of their day-to-day responsibilities, and they had to manage their commitments in order to accommodate it, as well as establish procedures for dealing with the many unscheduled demands on their time. Some detailed information about the nature of the work undertaken is given below, following a description of the backgrounds of those holding these five newly established posts.

Career backgrounds of the advisers and the establishment of their posts

Two of the newly appointed advisers and the advisory headteacher had taught in both mainstream and special schools prior to joining the advisory service. One had been a special school headteacher and then head of department in a college of further education; another had been deputy headteacher of a special school, and the third's most recent post had been as an advisory teacher for pupils with special educational needs. Their mainstream experience derived principally from teaching in secondary modern schools. The two advisers without special school teaching experience had entered this area of work through drama or physical education, and both had previously been advisers in one of these areas.

One adviser's career development was so closely aligned with the authority's deliberations that he could be viewed as instrumental in their decision-making. Originally an adviser for physical education in another authority, he had undertaken some work in special schools, 'as a matter of personal choice' and had then been given official responsibility for implementing the Education Act 1970 in the authority. Although he never taught in special schools he undertook a great deal of work with them in the capacity of adviser. When he joined his present authority in 1972 he had a particular brief to 'look after' probationary teachers in special education, being the only adviser with relevant experience. Responsibility for special education was 'tagged on as a temporary measure', but actually continued for some ten years without official recognition. The adviser advocated the need for a separate post from about 1978 because of the changing emphasis he perceived in special education reflecting the interest generated by the publication of the Warnock Report. When he applied for secondment to undertake a course concerned with pupils with special needs, his application was approved on the understanding that he would return to work as an adviser for special needs. In this way, a new post was created in 1983. There was no written job description and the job tended to develop in response to the wishes of the postholder.

The other adviser who came to special education through another subject joined the authority as a drama adviser during the 'big expansion' of 1974 when two advisers were appointed in every subject. Her belief in drama as a 'useful vehicle' for teaching pupils with special needs and her awareness of a 'gap in provision' for such pupils led to her applying for a transfer. Her new post as general adviser for educational needs and that of her colleague, as general adviser for special services, were established as a response to the 1981 Act to facilitate an expansion of the advisory service in relation to special needs. Previously there had been a general adviser with some responsibility for the special sector but this had been a 'special schools affair', and it had been decided to broaden the advisory service and establish new posts.

One of the other advisers said that following the 1981 Act there had been a 'mushrooming' of advertisements for special needs advisers in the educational press and his happened to be one of them. There had previously been advisers responsible for special schools but his post had been created to cater for 'that amorphous phrase "special educational needs" '. He understood that he had been appointed because of his broad mainstream and special school experience and said that he could not do the job effectively without having taught and handled problems in both special and mainstream schools.

The advisory headteacher described developments that had led to the establishment of three of these posts in her authority between 1980 and 1983. There had been a remedial service with advisory teachers who reported to the school psychological service and for several years the majority of schools each had a teacher receiving a special allowance who had particular responsibility for pupils with special needs. The new posts were created as part of a move to appoint staff to take overall responsibility for pupils with special needs. Psychologists were seen to have an increased administrative workload because of their commitment to preparing Statements, and the new posts were intended to provide an opportunity for teachers to receive advice from those 'who themselves had considerable teaching experience'.

The development of the advisory work

A common theme from the comments made by the advisers about their function was how loosely defined their work was. This sometimes resulted in staff undertaking tasks that were not officially recognized, and left individuals with considerable freedom to determine their own priorities. When the advisory headteachers were appointed they initially worked as a management team which received termly reports on progress. The advisory headteacher interviewed said that the group had not continued, and she was now included in the area team of administrators and advisers. Staff generally welcomed the freedom and flexibility provided by these arrangements and yet felt that a certain 'vulnerability' came with the responsibility. The adviser who had been actively involved with the establishment of his own post said that his responsibilities were advising as he chose, and that while this was rewarding it did 'create problems' in that it was essentially his responsibility to set priorities and decide how to spend his time. The advisory headteacher felt that her work could just consist of responding to requests made by others upon her time. When she was appointed she made very deliberate efforts to respond to requests from headteachers because she was aware that the new posts were viewed negatively in some instances and she wanted to change this perception. She experienced some difficulty in deciding exactly where she fitted into the team of colleagues; she had, for example, been involved in reviews undertaken by advisers until it had been pointed out to her by an education officer that these were not actually her responsibility.

One adviser spoke about the ever-present temptation in his job to 'react to situations'. Part of his solution was to write 'reserve' days into his diary to spend at special schools and to allocate time specifically to catch up on administrative tasks. He viewed the ability to be 'reactive' as an important feature of his work and suggested that the speed of reaction was important in helping people to handle situations themselves. An early response might be productive in helping participants to clarify a situation themselves. His new post had a 'momentum' of its own, and he anticipated that he would be 'run in' for about five years before his job was 'split' into different sections. There was great scope for diversity in the post and the adviser was keen to encourage growth while keeping 'a hand on the tiller'. There were advisory teachers in post, and he was able to exert considerable influence by working through them. As these teachers developed their role he could 'retreat' and become less involved. As the advisory post became established, he would be responsible for more staff and make a greater contribution to policy making.

Two advisers worked in an authority that employed them as general advisers working on an area basis for approximately 60 per cent of their workload. Developments within the authority had resulted in advisory colleagues not being replaced as they left, so that the demands of general advisory duties had expanded. Again, they stressed the numerous routine demands made on them which could easily have taken up all their time, and said that it was impossible to provide the sort of service they would have liked, given the number of schools they were responsible for. They were unable to spend as much time as they would have liked in schools and had developed a system of short visits combined with 'keeping their eyes open'.

Combining special and mainstream work

The new appointments in these authorities had all been made with an eye to providing for all pupils with special needs rather than as a means of supporting special school staff only. While the advisers differed in the finer details of their time allocation, all were clear that this more general responsibility was implicit in their post. The adviser who had returned from secondment to the newly created special needs post was in an unusual position in that he had previously worked in a different guise with all six special schools in the authority. His involvement with pupils with special needs had been confined to working in special schools where he had collaborated with staff in planning timetables, buying equipment, supervising teachers and appointing staff up to the level of deputy. Prior to his secondment he had not been involved with special education in mainstream schools and so was unaware of developments in special needs departments in relation to curriculum and staffing. Since taking up the new post he had been attempting to bridge that gap by making contact with mainstream schools. While the figures were approximate, this adviser estimated that he spent approximately 70 per cent of his time in special schools and 30 per cent in mainstream schools. He proposed a shift in this proportion so that he would be working in mainstream schools for 40 per cent of his time.

This adviser could identify a very subtle change of emphasis within his authority in relation to providing for pupils with special needs. For example, the role of special schools was changing in that they were developing as resource and support centres with equipment and expertise available to others. He saw himself as involved in arrangements concerning the remedial service and home tuition, because they were factors in developing a unified structure of provision. Another adviser described his responsibility as 'education in special schools and special needs in mainstream schools and all the other things that nobody else wanted'. He found it difficult to quantify how his time was spent in relation to the two sectors, and said that there was an element of 'crisis management' over and above the obvious areas of responsibility. He had pastoral oversight and general advisory responsibilities in the eight special schools in the borough and hoped to spend at least one full day a term in each of them. He could generally commit only half a day at a time to other activities but did try to keep these all-day sessions free for the special schools. He could identify large-scale changes in providing for pupils with special needs that would be introduced very gradually and said that he had already encountered considerable changes in attitude. There was a sense of schools 'coming together', and staff were generally more involved and interested in special education and were becoming rather better informed. This adviser's perception of his role as having a broad base gave him a central role in influencing these developments.

The advisory headteacher for special needs reported that, although she did not spend a great deal of time in the four special schools in her area, she did have a fairly substantial commitment to them, as she had expected from the job description given for her post. She was also involved in working with the eight special classes in her area. There were increasing numbers of ancillary workers supporting pupils with Statements in ordinary schools, and supervising these arrangements was part of her task. She referred also to 'a great deal of discussion with special school headteachers about the role that they might play in the future'.

She mentioned the development of special schools as resource and support centres and said that it was extremely difficult for special school teachers to translate their specialist knowledge into terms that were meaningful to a class teacher who had 30 pupils, including one with special educational needs. While the changes in provision inevitably had an effect on the advisory headteacher's work, she did feel that her allocated duties were as she had anticipated, in that a significant responsibility was the supervision of the advisory and peripatetic teachers in her area. These staff were providing support and resources for mainstream staff, as well as teaching individual children.

The two advisers in one authority who had general posts with special educational needs and special services respectively added on, worked to a senior adviser of special services. The former was concerned with special educational provision in mainstream schools and was also responsible for two centres for disruptive pupils. These centres were of particular interest to her and had been added to her list of responsibilities, as had the education of gifted children and travellers. The other adviser had responsibility for special schools and units, and for children with special needs between birth and five years old, in addition to his general advisory duties. There were more than 20 special schools and eight units in the authority, and although each had a general adviser, the special services adviser played a complementary specialized role. His work was influenced by a concern to develop the curriculum in the special schools and by potential new roles for them in the light of the 1981 Act. He felt that there would need to be a response to falling rolls in these schools, and he was involved in discussing possible changes with staff. He also had some contact with the services for hearing and visually impaired pupils.

The advisers' schedules

While the advisers may have been clear about their responsibilities and priorities, and the balance they were aiming for between work in special and mainstream schools, they all stressed the erratic and demanding nature of their work. The two general advisers with specialist responsibilities tried to visit their 'general' schools at least twice a term, and were quite clear that their workload was 'excessive'. Another adviser spoke of the 'dilemma' he faced in finding enough time to deal with the considerable amount of paperwork his job involved. He saw his work as being very much 'out in the field' and spent a lot of time visiting schools. He was aware that some people thought his work was 'a real skive' because he was sometimes difficult to contact. He saw this sort of criticism as 'part of the job' and just tried to keep on achieving his aims.

One adviser who stressed that her working routine was very flexible, detailed her division of time for the previous week. She had recorded 49 hours of work, which did not include time spent travelling. There had been ten hours' visiting schools, which was an unusually low figure, and another ten hours had been spent at her desk in the office. There were 11 hours allocated for work on in-service training and three hours for miscellaneous duties. The eight hours used up by committees and meetings were more than would be usual. The remaining hours had been time spent at home writing up notes and tidying up business at the end of the day.

To illustrate the diversity of his work, another adviser provided information about how four recent working days had been spent. He arrived at the office around 7.45 am to deal with correspondence and during the morning had a meeting with advisory colleagues about curriculum development. The afternoon was spent interviewing staff for a special school and he returned to the office at around 6.15 pm to undertake paperwork. The evening was spent at a governors' meeting at a special school. The early part of the next day was spent on administration, but the bulk of the day was taken up by a routine visit to a residential school. He concluded with an hour's administration in the office. The third day had a similar pattern, with school hours being spent as a 'reserve' day in a special school. There was a meeting about Portage at 4.15 pm and another governors' meeting in the evening. The last day also began with paperwork, followed by a visit to a junior school to talk about a child with behaviour problems who had been causing concern. The bulk of the day consisted of another 'reserved' visit to a special school, and from 4–6 pm he was involved in an in-service session on behaviour management for the home tuition team.

Aspects of the advisers' work

The advisers interviewed indicated certain central aspects of their work that were common to all posts. They all identified an element that could be termed support and management, and there was developmental work undertaken that included committee and in-service commitments. They all referred to the administrative duties their posts carried. Contributing to assessment and Statementing procedures formed part of this task. These different aspects are discussed separately below.

Support and management

One adviser explicitly referred to providing support to teachers, headteachers and parents as a priority in his work. He occasionally dealt directly with parents, particularly when they were concerned about a placement, but his support for them was usually indirect through schools and agencies. He referred to a recent traumatic period for staff and pupils in one special school and said that his function then had been to support individuals in the school and to secure the services of a trained counsellor. This was typical of his approach, which involved identifying a need and contacting somebody who would be able to help. He saw his work with the special schools as being to advise in any way that seemed appropriate and occasionally to act as a catalyst for change. He described what he was to do the following morning and said that it was fairly typical. He was to visit a primary school that would be taking a girl with Down's Syndrome the following year. The staff had no experience of this type of child and he was going along essentially to reassure them that they could cope. The word 'reassure' was used frequently when he described his daily contacts. After that he was to visit a secondary school to discuss the curriculum with staff in the remedial department.

The two advisers with both general and specialist responsibilities were concerned by what they saw as very low morale among teaching staff and felt that the counselling, supportive dimension of their work had come to the fore. The adviser who worked in mainstream schools said that although she saw herself as a catalyst in schools there was currently so much counselling attached to her work that this tended to dominate. Both advisers felt that they were striving to keep up the morale of schools and that they must continue to provide a very 'professional service'.

There was considerable variation in the managerial responsibilities given to the advisers and this reflected the different policies of their authorities. Their relationship with the support services was one example: while some advisers had clear managerial responsibility for this provision, others saw it as 'the preserve' of the school psychological service. One adviser, for example, had no formal commitment to the service, but did have the responsibility to inspect it occasionally and was involved in clarifying the direction that this form of provision should take. The advisory headteacher, by contrast, had responsibility for all the advisory and peripatetic teachers for pupils with special needs in her authority. There was also a different emphasis with regard to the proportion of time spent on pupils with special needs in ordinary schools, though in all the authorities there were clear indications that the advisory service was intended to promote a broad definition of special educational needs.

In addition, the advisers were involved to various degrees in related areas of educational provision, ranging from home tuition to visiting independent schools which provided for children in their authority. A considerable part of the advisory headteacher's work was concerned with managing the advisory and peripatetic teachers. She also had a role in the unit for maladjusted pupils, provision for travellers' children and education provided in hospital. She provided support for home tutors in relation to the curriculum and had responsibility for monitoring pupils who had ancillary help in mainstream schools.

In-service training

When the advisers spoke about their in-service work for teachers it was clear that their areas of responsibility were very broad. They were presenting courses of varying lengths on a variety of topics for staff in both ordinary and special schools. Their responsibility for providing support for staff in ordinary schools was perhaps most evident in this aspect of their work.

One adviser, for example, referred in detail to the support he had given to staff in remedial departments in devising their work plans in connection with the one-term courses introduced as part of the new in-service training arrangements in 1983. He was gratified by the increasing awareness that he perceived in teachers of their responsibility for the curriculum, and was eager to provide them with assistance to develop this work. He stressed that he was not seeking to 'de-skill' teachers but rather to help them to apply the skills they already had. He expected to spend roughly equal amounts of time on in-service work in special and ordinary schools and envisaged organizing seminars for staff in the former. This adviser suggested that there were elements of training in much of his work because he was responsible for supervising anybody who was pursuing any line of enquiry concerned with special educational needs. He would be approached for advice when teachers were seeking secondments relating to special needs, and he was conscious of being a source of advice and a 'sounding board' for staff considering these activities. He had established in-service work with the remedial support team on three afternoons a term and was working with them to look at the particular difficulties children might have and the best approaches that could be taken to deal with them. He had also initiated a course for more than 30 key mainstream staff to consider a set of modules concerned with the early identification of children with hearing difficulties.

The two general advisers with specialist responsibilities were both enthusiastic about the potential benefits to be derived from in-service training and clearly awarded it priority in their work. The adviser concerned primarily with ordinary schools was critical of the attitude she perceived in some staff, that if they were allocated extra teachers they would be able to provide much more effectively for their pupils with special needs. She regarded this as 'far too simplistic' because 'they weren't on top of the situation anyway'. In-service training was perceived as a way of maximizing what was currently available in schools. These two advisers had organized some residential courses together; they saw these as opportunities for promoting certain innovations that they wanted to see developed in schools. The emphasis was on informing and attempting to persuade. One adviser gave the example of team teaching in this context and said that they had tried to illustrate the benefits of this form of organization and to 'point out that once people had done it they were very enthusiastic about it'.

The adviser working in ordinary schools tended to focus on school-based work in the secondary schools, where she was attempting to instigate a 'whole-school' approach to meeting special educational needs. She was concerned at the tremendous variation she saw in how effectively secondary schools catered for their pupils with special needs, and said that there was certainly 'a lack of understanding' among staff in some schools. She planned to approach this first by holding a staff conference in the school. The general adviser who had a specialist commitment to special schools said that he actively encouraged staff to take secondment and was pleased that the opportunities were now there for many staff. He was particularly keen for this to be taken up in schools that were not developing networks with other schools or becoming established as resource centres. His main commitment to in-service training was holding courses in the teachers' centre.

One adviser described an initiative undertaken with remedial departments in secondary schools and viewed this as the approach that would be most productive, given his brief. The course began with one full-day session followed by two half-day sessions in the same term and several evening sessions of one and a half to two hours during the school year. It officially ended with two half-day sessions at the end of the school year. The adviser was extremely pleased that there had been some 'spin-off', in that development groups had been formed by participants that met on their own initiative to discuss specific issues. This form of collective response was vital to the development of whole-school policies, he felt, because it was important that people could 'sit down and discuss how they might approach the maths department, for example'. Another initiative intended for ordinary school staff with no qualifications in special needs had been heavily over-subscribed and had been run twice. The six sessions were designed to assist teachers in observing and identifying children with special needs, and there was an emphasis on practical sessions and discussion groups. More specifically, the adviser had initiated school-based work at schools for pupils with moderate learning difficulties because he was 'keen to introduce ideas to them' and wanted to help teachers to clarify what they were doing.

The advisory headteacher described her responsibility to special schools as being to arrange in-service training and to respond to any request they might make: she was involved in in-service work with the advisory and peripatetic staff. They ran a course lasting for 12 hours spread out over a year for mainstream teachers with special allowances. She had also been instrumental in establishing contact groups so that teachers working with pupils with special needs could meet to discuss areas of common concern. They met termly and sometimes had invited speakers. She was one of four members of a planning group concerned with residential courses for special school staff that met four times a year.

Developing provision

One common theme raised by the advisers interviewed was that they were frequently involved in discussions with special school headteachers about developments in their schools. One, indeed, was interviewed directly after one such meeting, which had been called because the authority 'agreed in principle with the 1981 Act' and wished to move towards its intentions. Another adviser had been concerned with deliberations in special schools with regard to falling rolls. He had concentrated on bringing staff in schools together to discuss the issues and had been instrumental in the authority's awards of £1000 to each of 12 special schools.

The initiatives in which the advisers were involved were often very clearly dependent on additional resources. One adviser described the working parties on which she had sat, and said that they had been established to find solutions to areas of concern to the Education Committee. She referred to one that had been set up to investigate the centres for pupils with behaviour problems for which she was responsible, and said that there had been far-reaching recommendations. The working party had estimated that approximately £300,000 would be required to implement the changes, but in fact only the equivalent of five full-time teachers had been allocated. She reported having made 'very strong bids' to obtain resources for travellers' children and had put in a lot of effort to acquire the two vans they had been allocated. This adviser certainly saw herself as advocating increased expenditure on these groups of pupils in a consistent way. She was, for example, on the Suspension from School panel and felt that 'nobody wanted to know about these pupils' until she 'started making a noise about it'. She had direct access to a very small fund that could be used as and when required, but this had recently been cut by 30 per cent.

Apart from this, the advisers interviewed were generally unaware of or not involved in the processes of financial management and were sometimes frustrated by their inability to influence the allocation of resources. Two advisers in an authority which had recently employed a substantial number of new teachers to work in primary schools felt that their professional advice had not been sufficiently considered, and were not aware of the criteria for decision-making that had been used by the Education Committee. They both felt it would have been appropriate for them to be more directly involved in the allocation of finance. One said that when he took up his post he had felt that his advice was 'being listened to', but he was now very concerned about the lack of consultation with professionals that he discerned.

One adviser felt he did have influence when he argued for certain facilities to be provided. He would make a request to the education officers and he was frequently asked to comment on requests received from other individuals. He regarded 'making a case and solidifying the arguments for the elected members' as very much part of his work. Another adviser reported that any discussions about financing special educational provision included him. He also had a small equipment fund that he could use directly. He had recently, for example, purchased a micro-writer for one boy and a page-turner for a girl.

The influence of financial arrangements on the work of advisers was illustrated by the position of the advisory headteacher. The advisory teachers for whom she was responsible had had approximately 50 per cent of their time allocated for teaching, but because the service was to be reduced in the near future their role would change. The advisory headteacher would be working with staff to facilitate this change of emphasis in their work. The schools would be expected to take on more direct responsibility for the pupils on their rolls and the advisory staff would work with them on identifying and assessing pupils rather than on giving direct assistance. This advisory headteacher saw herself as having a developmental role in relation to the service, in that she was trying to reduce the number of schools for which they were responsible and to establish a service of enthusiastic and well-qualified staff.

Professional relationships

In some respects the advisers saw their work as very much an individual and self-motivated activity, but there were also many activities arranged with other colleagues, and much of the work involved considerable contact with others. One adviser, for example, said that he worked very independently from his advisory colleagues and had little regular involvement with them. He was responsible to the director, through the chief inspector, and described all other relationships as 'sideways'. He worked directly with a senior assistant education officer and met with him and the principal educational psychologist every two months. There was contact with other psychologists as appropriate, particularly in relation to in-service work. This independence coupled with contact with advisory colleagues was elaborated on by the other advisers. One said that he certainly felt part of the team of 12; there was a very productive atmosphere where problems were shared. If he felt that a school for which he was responsible could usefully receive advice about home economics, for example, he would contact the appropriate adviser and request a visit. By this means he felt that they 'hunted together well'. The advisory headteacher said that she was working at encouraging all advisers to see work with special schools as part of their brief, and she would have liked the headteachers in these schools to draw upon the expertise of subject advisers more than they currently did.

The two general advisers with specialist responsibilities said that, while it was extremely difficult to arrange meetings with other colleagues in the Education Office because of the pressure of time, they did have productive relationships with their advisory colleagues. Advisers in their division met monthly and they had their own in-service training days that were extremely productive. They certainly felt that they had a team of colleagues they could contact and that they did collaborate when required.

Administration

A common theme in the interviews conducted with the advisers was the difficulties encountered in dealing with the considerable amount of administration involved in their work. One said, for example, that he estimated that about 25 per cent of his work was 'office-bound', whereas he would like it to be as little as five per cent. Allocating time to these duties did pose a 'dilemma'. There were crucial elements in this work including writing reports, attending meetings and presenting the case for new developments. He was conscious that he could reasonably be criticized for his slow response to certain administrative tasks, but he did not feel motivated to deal with them as a priority. His work was very much 'out in the field' and he spent a great deal of time in schools. Another adviser expressed his surprise on coming into the advisory service from higher education to find that there was so little administrative 'back-up'. He felt that many of his tasks could have been delegated to others, and it seemed inappropriate that 'someone with experience and expertise who was paid a good deal of money was then expected to do mundane clerking'. The amount of paperwork and the number of telephone calls the adviser received were 'excessive' so that a 'balancing act' had to be performed to reconcile the conflicting demands placed upon them.

An important part of the administrative workload of these advisers was the preparation of assessments and Statements. They were all involved to varying degrees, and for two of them the involvement was considerable. The two general advisers in one authority said that it had initially been agreed that only one of them would be involved in the Statementing procedures along with the senior adviser who was the Statementing Officer. However, the volume of work had become so great that the other adviser had been drawn in to undertake the Statements for children in high schools. This had subsequently been extended to cover the age range from five to 18. This work was described as 'an inordinate administrative burden' by one of them.

The advisory headteacher worked with a colleague in preparing Statements for pre-school children. Her only involvement with older children was that she was sometimes asked to chair case conferences and meetings. She did feel that hers was 'a name that headteachers knew' if they had any points to make about Statements. Another adviser said that he was not involved in the process of Statementing, but he was involved in the outcomes, in that he was consulted about placements. He sometimes worked with parents where there were potential disagreements about the outcome of a Statement. Another adviser described the process of 'negotiated Statementing' that existed in his authority. He was very much involved in the writing of Statements 'because it was seen as a curriculum matter', and he worked with the principal educational psychologist and the assistant director for schools on this. He described Statements as 'instruments for looking in detail at the curricular needs of individuals' and said that his involvement illustrated the way in which he worked as a team member with psychologists and administrators.

6 The New Special Needs Support and Advisory Service

Developments in 'remedial' provision

Each of the 77 authorities surveyed operated a support service to assist pupils with learning difficulties and their teachers in ordinary schools. There was considerable variation in the size and organization of the services, in the type of assistance offered and in the number and range of pupils catered for. A number of authorities reported that since 1978 they had been making changes which were broadly in line with the Warnock Report, which recommended that 'every local education authority should restructure and if necessary supplement its existing advisory staff and resources to provide effective advice and support to teachers concerned with children with special educational needs *through a unified support service*' (13:3).

Sixty-six per cent of the LEAs reported that they had achieved major innovations in their support services. Invariably the remedial reading service was at the centre of the re-thinking and re-organization. Although, for the most part, the changes were in the same general direction, there were considerable variations between authorities.

At the time of publication of the Warnock Report in 1978, the majority of authorities ran some sort of remedial reading service, in some instances of long standing, and in others established in response to the Bullock Report of 1975. This same year saw wholesale changes in local government organization and many authorities took the opportunity to establish new services in the reorganized, and in some cases newly created, local authorities. The following characteristics were typical of most services:

- the concentration was exclusively, or at least predominantly, upon reading problems;
- the service was principally for primary schools;
- most, if not all staff of the service taught children with reading problems directly, usually in small groups but sometimes individually; and,
- children were withdrawn from the classroom for this extra help, which was usually given within the school but sometimes at a separate reading centre.

All of these characteristics, and the working practices associated with them, were subjected to much criticism. Indeed, the whole notion of remedial education had been called into question. The major criticism was that the term 'remedial', with its medical overtones, suggested that there was something wrong with the child that needed a remedy. The strong implication was that the source of the difficulties lay entirely in the child: that the child was suffering from some defect which prevented him or her from achieving normal progress in a school system that, even if capable of improvement, was basically sound. It was the child who was 'remedial' and in need of treatment, not the school. 'Remedial' became a pejorative label. The appropriateness of this perspective was increasingly challenged following Golby and Gulliver's (1979) argument that it was the curriculum, and indeed the whole education system, that should be regarded as defective, rather than the child. This view became more widespread and was reflected in several studies of schooling for pupils with special educational needs (Tomlinson, 1982). It created a climate of opinion in which more people were thinking in terms of modifying the school, or at least the curriculum, to suit the child, rather than the other way around.

Just as 'remedial' implied that there was something wrong with the child, it also suggested that there was a cure. Warnock pointed out that this was often not the case. Remedial groups in schools included children with a variety of difficulties which, though very different in origin, were often treated as if they were alike. Some of these difficulties might be temporary, but others were of a more permanent nature.

> It is true that some of them are suffering only a temporary learning difficulty and, given appropriate help, are able to return rapidly to their previous classes, having completely overcome their disability. Others, however, require special help and support throughout their school lives and to say that these children require 'remedial' education is misleading (Warnock Report, 3:39).

Warnock went on to recommend that the distinction commonly made between 'remedial' and 'special' education should cease because, in the context of the new concept of special educational needs, the distinction was no longer meaningful. The declared intention was that children who had previously been ascertained as requiring special education, together with children in the remedial departments of ordinary schools, should, in future, all be regarded as children with special educational needs for whom some form of special provision should be made. The changes in provision that would follow this change in thinking would require very different sorts of provision to be made in ordinary schools. There would have to be a recognition that the bulk of the work of the special needs department in future would revolve around providing continued support across the curriculum for pupils who would need this help for the whole of their school lives. This was a very different task from trying to offer a 'cure' to pupils who had reading problems.

The proposed changes were undoubtedly radical and involved very different working practices for those directly involved, but they seem to have been well-received, and school remedial departments and local authority remedial support services generally responded positively. There were, perhaps, two main reasons for this. First and most important, Warnock's recommendations did in fact reflect changes that were already beginning to take place in the world of remedial education. Secondly, the proposed changes offered the prospect of higher prestige and an expansion of opportunities for teachers working in what had often previously been regarded as the poor relation of the education service.

In the mid-1970s, the National Association for Remedial Education (NARE) was debating, very seriously, the whole future of remedial work in schools. Cutbacks and the threat of such at that time made remedial teachers feel particularly vulnerable. Their service was commonly regarded as a low prestige area of work and the heads of remedial departments in schools were rarely on comparable scales to the subject department heads (Clunies-Ross and Wimhurst, 1983). Much of the remedial work, particularly in primary schools, was done by part-time teachers who were most vulnerable to local authority economies (Croll and Moses, 1985). In addition, there was a growing body of literature which suggested that remedial education as then practised was not particularly successful in producing long-term gains in performance. All these factors encouraged NARE to examine carefully the purposes, practices and prospects of remedial education. The proceedings of their 1977 conference (Gains and McNicholas, 1981) stressed the need for a new direction, and recommended that remedial teachers should strive for the earliest possible identification of children who were likely to experience difficulties, with a focus on prevention rather than cure where at all feasible. Remedial work should also be seen as an activity carried out across the whole curriculum, not one which concentrated exclusively on English. Against this background, the recommendations of the Warnock Report were, for the most part, welcomed by practitioners in remedial education.

The position of teachers in special schools was rather different. Their expertise in teaching children with special needs was not seriously questioned but the future of their schools often gave them cause for concern. Although Warnock had clearly stated that special schools would continue to be needed to provide education for some children into the foreseeable future, there were fears that if authorities, following Warnock and perhaps under pressure from parents, actively pursued policies of placing more children in ordinary schools, this would inevitably lead to the closure of at least some special schools. (The present research suggests that, although there have not been wholesale closures of special schools across the country, numbers of pupils in special education are now falling and some special schools are closing.) In practical as well as ideological terms, the way ahead for the special education sector appeared to lie in closer contact with ordinary schools and particularly with the departments of ordinary schools closest to special education, i.e. the remedial departments. The blurring or disappearance of distinctions between remedial and special education opened the door to new opportunities.

The changing ideas about the nature of remedial work inevitably had major implications in practice. The old-style service had been based on the assumption that the central problem was that some children experienced great difficulties in learning to read adequately and that this problem had to be remedied before they could gain access to the rest of the curriculum. It was generally assumed that children would have learnt to read adequately by the time they reached the age of eight or nine, if not before, so that failure to have mastered good reading skills became an increasingly serious problem as the pupils got older. Because pupils who could not read to the level demanded in the classroom had problems there, it appeared to make sense that they should be withdrawn, either individually or in small groups, for specialist help with reading. If this remediation worked and the pupils could master the required skills and participate in school work with their peers, then this procedure could be regarded as being successful.

It is perhaps worth bearing in mind that, although for many children it is desirable to see support as being long-term and their difficulties not subject to any 'cure', there are other children with a variety of short-term difficulties that can be overcome. The term 'remedial' may, in some respects, be an inadequate and misleading concept, but it does, nevertheless, have a desirable optimism about it. It may not be helpful to look for a cure that does not exist, but it is essential to maintain a belief that at least a proportion of children will, with the right help, overcome their problems.

The support services as they currently operate

Despite the debate over the whole notion of remedial education, and the questioning of the appropriateness of the term to describe the activity undertaken, 'remedial' still frequently appeared in the title of the support service. Thirty-eight per cent of the authorities in the survey used the term 'remedial', though 'remedial reading' only appeared in three cases. A very wide range of titles was given to the support services catering for children with learning difficulties in ordinary schools, perhaps because their range of activities was also very varied. Titles chosen for the service included Learning Difficulties Support Service, Special Education Support Service, Support Service for Pupils with Special Educational Needs, Advisory Teacher Service and Special Education Support Team. Different names probably do indicate some differences in the scope and emphases of services, but it would be wrong to read too much significance into mere titles.

Budgeting for the service

A service concerned with special educational needs in ordinary schools cuts across the boundaries between special and ordinary education in a very obvious way. This is particularly so in the case of assistance offered to pupils who are the subject of Statements, and is reflected in the variety of budgeting arrangements made for the service.

Table 6.1: *Is the service funded from the special education budget?*

	LEAs	%
Yes	32	41.5
No	37	48.1
Don't know	7	9.1
Other	1	1.3
Total	77	100.0

As indicated in Table 6.1, the authorities were fairly evenly divided between those who financed the support service from the special education budget and those who did not. Only one authority operated a joint primary/special education budget, and there was no indication that other authorities were intending to establish joint budgets. Most of the authorities that did not use the special education budget operated the service from the primary schools budget, which may indicate that although secondary schools were coming within the orbit of the support service increasingly often, their clients had traditionally been primary pupils and the emphasis of their work was still on the younger age groups. Authorities were not asked about changes that had been made in budgeting arrangements but three volunteered the information that the funding of the support service had been moved into the special education budget because this budget was viewed as less likely to be subject to expenditure cuts.

Running the service

Table 6.2: *To whom is the head of the service responsible?*

	LEAs	%
Education officer	30	39.0
Adviser for special educational needs	20	26.0
Officer/adviser jointly	13	16.9
Principal educational psychologist	14	18.1
Total	77	100.0

It is perhaps surprising that the principal educational psychologist was in charge of only 18 per cent of services. Educational psychologists work in both ordinary and special schools and are in an advantageous position for bringing special and ordinary education closer together. However, the trend was away from the school psychological service controlling the support service towards a situation where the head of service was directly responsible to an officer. Education officers, of varying degrees of seniority, were solely in charge of 39 per cent of services and, in conjunction with the adviser for special educational needs, of a further 17 per cent. The advisers for special educational needs also had sole control of 26 per cent of services. (In two cases the principal educational psychologist was also the adviser for special educational needs. In these instances he was regarded as a psychologist as, in both cases, this was the original post to which the additional title and responsibilities had been added.)

Staffing the service

Table 6.3: *Numbers of advisory teachers, peripatetic teachers and support staff in the LEAs*

No. of staff	*LEAs*	%
Up to 10	17	22.0
11–20	14	18.2
20–30	24	31.2
30–40	2	2.6
40–50	3	3.9
50+	9	11.7
Unknown	8	10.4
Total	77	100.0

A number of factors appear to have influenced the size of the service besides the size of the authority and the overall level of resourcing for this type of provision. Some of the largest shire county authorities had very small services, and some small metropolitan authorities and London boroughs had comparatively large ones. An important determining factor was the nature of the service offered. Services that were solely or predominantly concerned with advising teachers in schools tended to be much smaller than those that taught children directly. This difference was also reflected in the number of higher grade staff employed. Services that were predominantly teaching services tended to have a large number of staff, the vast majority of whom were Scale 1 or Scale 2 teachers, whereas services that were predominantly advisory were often staffed exclusively by teachers who held Scale 3 or more senior posts. However, there was an enormous variation in the seniority of staff doing seemingly the same job in different authorities. A striking example is provided by contrasting the grading of two heads of service. In one London borough the head of service was paid as a Group 6 headteacher while the head of service in a shire county, with a school population four times as large, was paid as a Scale 4 teacher.

Table 6.4: *Changes in staffing levels since 1978*

	LEAs	%
Overall increase	42	54.5
Overall decrease	11	14.3
No overall change	19	24.7
Unknown	5	6.5
Total	77	100.0

Over half the authorities had had an overall increase in staff. Some of these increases were very substantial, involving the appointment of as many as 30 new professional staff. Nearly a quarter of authorities reported no overall change but this frequently disguised substantial reorganization mostly in the direction of a reduction in the number of peripatetic teachers who taught children directly, and an increase in advisory teachers. The services that reported an overall decrease in staff numbers appeared also to be moving towards a more advisory role and reducing their peripatetic teaching staff.

Contact with ordinary and special schools

Tables 6.5 and 6.6 indicate the time spent by the support service staff in ordinary schools and in special schools and units. The most significant finding is the limited amount of contact that most services had with special schools. It is perhaps surprising that they did not put more time and effort into drawing ordinary and special schools together to share expertise and experience. Nearly a half of the services had no contact at all with special schools and units, and a further 20 per cent spent five per cent or less of their time in the special schools. Just three services spent between a quarter and a half of their time in special schools and units. In these cases the services were based in, and provided staff, for a unit as well as offering a service of support to ordinary schools. This was an arrangement that was common practice in provision for pupils with sensory impairments but unusual in provision for pupils with learning difficulties.

Table 6.5: *Proportion of time that the service spends in ordinary schools*

% time spent in ordinary schools	*LEAs*	*%*
90–100	44	57.1
75–89	11	14.3
50–74	14	18.2
Under 50	2	2.6
Unknown	6	7.8
Total	77	100.0

Table 6.6: *Contacts with special schools and units*

% time spent in special schools and units	*LEAs*	*%*
None	36	46.7
1–5	16	20.8
6–25	17	22.1
26–50	3	3.9
Unknown	5	6.5
Total	77	100.0

Helping teachers and teaching pupils

Only two authorities reported that their service dealt exclusively with teachers, and just one said that the service which they operated worked entirely with pupils. All the other services divided their time between pupils and teachers.

Although there had been an increase in the advisory function of the support services, it can be seen from Table 6.7 that most services still spent the bulk of their time teaching children. Over 63 per cent of the services spent more than half their time, and over 40 per cent spent more than three-quarters of their time teaching. Nearly 17 per cent spent more than half their time working with teachers, while just over ten per cent spent at least three-quarters of their time in this way. It is perhaps significant that nearly 20 per cent of services were not able to say how their time was divided between teaching and advising – which indicates that staff had a certain amount of flexibility in responding to different school situations.

Table 6.7: *Time spent with pupils in ordinary schools*

% time in ordinary schools spent with pupils	*LEAs*	*%*
75+	31	40.2
50–74	18	23.4
25–49	5	6.5
Under 25	8	10.4
Unknown	15	19.5
Total	77	100.0

The selection of pupils for help

Authority-wide screening formed the basis for the selection of pupils for extra help in 72.2 per cent (61) of the responding authorities, but no service relied exclusively on screening test results alone. In all instances, although the test results were regarded as having supplied valuable information, the decision about whether or not a child would receive help from the support service also depended upon the opinions of the teachers concerned and frequently on the judgements of educational psychologists and advisers. In those authorities that did not conduct screening tests, children were selected for help by a combination of request from the school and recommendation from either an educational psychologist or an adviser. There was only one exception to this rule: one metropolitan authority allocated assistance on the basis of school request alone.

With the emphasis changing from direct help for the pupil to support and advice for the teacher, it proved difficult to gauge with any accuracy how many children were receiving help. As many as 41.5 per cent of authorities could not say how many children were being helped by the service and a further 28.6 per cent could only give approximate figures.

Although the exact number of children being helped was often unclear, it was apparent that no service aimed to reach directly all pupils estimated to have special needs. A few of the largest services claimed to reach 10–12 per cent of the junior age group, but most catered for a very much smaller number of pupils. It was very evident that the needs of most pupils still had to be met by their class teachers and that advice was all the help that many teachers could expect.

Withdrawal

The traditional way for pupils to receive remedial help was through withdrawal from the regular classroom for help in a smaller group. The practice of withdrawal has recently been the subject of growing criticism, being attacked from many quarters, although not always for sound reasons. A new orthodoxy would appear to be developing in which help in the classroom is seen as the only solution, and withdrawal is regarded as positively undesirable. However, despite the increasing criticism, withdrawal without doubt has remained popular with junior school teachers. Both Croll and Moses (1985) and Gipps *et al.* (1987) found that teachers regarded withdrawal as the most useful type of help that could be provided for children with learning difficulties and they would like to see this provision extended to more pupils.

Three authorities in the current research emphasized that the help that they offered directly to pupils was always in the classroom, never through withdrawal. In marked contrast, just one authority said that it had a policy of always withdrawing children from the classroom. All the rest used a mixture of support within the classroom and withdrawal but unfortunately the proportion of withdrawal to other help was generally not known. Many support services reported a move away from withdrawal, but, as we have seen, only three services rejected it entirely as a practice. Where children were withdrawn from the classroom for remedial help, on the whole the support services operated in schools rather than in other centres. Sixteen services undertook a proportion of their work with children in non-school settings but none operated exclusively outside schools. The general picture that emerged was that children with special educational needs were still frequently withdrawn from the classroom for special help but it was relatively unusual for them to leave the school.

Despite the strong body of opinion opposed to withdrawal, classroom practitioners were still firmly in favour of this method of teaching. Advisory and support services which wish to move away from this model of support may well face a distinct lack of enthusiasm from schools, and they will need to be very clear about their reasons for rejecting this popular practice.

It would probably also be a mistake to encourage the pendulum to swing too far away from reading problems. It is right to recognize that pupils experience a variety of learning difficulties. Reading is only one area where problems occur and other difficulties deserve attention. It is also right to point out that there are means of access to the curriculum other than the printed word and these may be highly beneficial for those children for whom reading remains a barrier. Nevertheless, reading will continue to be of the utmost importance. Children, and adults too, who have not mastered reading skills will still be seriously disadvantaged. The adult literacy campaign brought to the public attention just how many adults could not read and how this disability caused serious hardship in their lives. It proved possible to teach many of those who asked for help to read adequately. They did not suffer from an incurable condition, but one that could, and did, respond to remediation. All schools want their pupils to be literate before they leave. It is essential that other learning difficulties are catered for and that realistic, rather than impossible, goals are set for pupils, but the centrality of reading and its importance for all pupils must not be forgotten.

Changes in the support service

The major changes that have been made in the support service for pupils with learning difficulties in ordinary schools can be summarized as follows: the teacher is now a client of the service as well as the pupil; there is a greater orientation towards offering help in the classroom as opposed to withdrawing pupils from it; and a wider range of special needs than simply reading difficulties are being dealt with.

Just over 20 per cent of authorities surveyed had merged previously existing support services to form a single all-encompassing service. Although in most instances such services catered for pupils both with and without Statements, in three authorities a separate service operated for pupils in ordinary schools with Statements. It seems that in these cases it had been possible to abandon the rigidity of the categories of handicap but not the distinction between ordinary and special education! Nevertheless, the overall picture was one of closer cooperation between all those involved in offering help through the support service to pupils and teachers in ordinary schools.

The new special needs advisory and support service – a case study

Many of the issues involved in the establishment of a new-style generic support service can be illuminated by looking in detail at the development of such a service in a shire county which we shall call

Brentonshire. This particular scheme does not incorporate all possible changes and cannot be regarded as 'typical'. Neither is it used as a model of good practice, although there is no denying that it has many desirable characteristics. The purpose is to look closely at an instance of this type of change in action. At numerous points practice in Brentonshire will be compared and contrasted with practice in other authorities.

Outline of changes

The change that has been accomplished involved the transformation of the Remedial Reading Service (RRS) into the Special Educational Needs Advisory and Support Service (SENASS), which includes services for the hearing and visually impaired and education for children not at school. Instead of support to ordinary schools being limited to help given in the form of direct teaching to junior age children with reading problems, teaching help and advice is now offered to all types of schools and caters for the whole range of special educational needs.

Background

Although it would not be appropriate to include a blow-by-blow account of events over the last 15 years or so, it is worth considering the significance of the establishment of the new local authority in 1974. As part of the reorganization of local government, the county of Brentonshire changed significantly. Not only was the city of Brenton, with its rather different educational policies, incorporated into the county, but a large area of the southern part of the shire was lost when it was incorporated into a newly created authority. The magnitude of this change can be appreciated when the size and population of the present county are compared with the past. In 1973, Brentonshire covered 326,048 hectares and had a population of 1,109,000, while ten years later in 1983 it had been reduced to 264,266 hectares with a population of only 507,600. The decline in size in 1974 was not immediately matched by a corresponding scaling down of services, so although provision in most areas of education has been the subject of economies in recent years, these have been made from a fairly high base.

Before 1974 special education was the responsibility of a third tier education officer who was also responsible for primary education; reorganization and restructuring did not change this situation. It is significant that the growing interest in special educational needs that preceded the Warnock Report resulted in this aspect of education becoming more separate, rather than part of an integrated administration. In 1977, a new post of senior education officer for special education and personal services was created, indicating a recognition of the increased importance of special education. This officer, together with the adviser for special education, was largely responsible for the changes in special needs provision.

The remedial reading service

Brentonshire had for many years operated a remedial reading service which although engaging in many traditional practices also incorporated several very unusual features. The new service grew out of this old service, using many of its existing staff and much of its organization. Change was achieved and is continuing through a process of gradual adaptation which could sometimes be speeded up by making the most of favourable circumstances when they presented themselves. In this authority change was seen by the officers and advisers to be a gradual process that had to take account of past and present practices and personnel in post. There were no sudden closures of services, with the associated loss of posts, followed by the establishment of new kinds of support services with different staffing bases, as described in Chapter 3.

Before the establishment of SENASS, the county operated a remedial reading service which was staffed by a head of service, eight advisory teachers and 56.25 full-time equivalent remedial teachers, virtually all of whom were part-time. The service offered assistance to pupils in primary schools and, although it allowed for some flexibility, this help usually consisted of the direct teaching of reading to small withdrawal groups of first-, second- and third-year juniors. Help was rarely extended to fourth-year juniors because, it was argued, these pupils would have to get accustomed to managing without this type of help when they went to secondary schools.

The authority operated a county-wide screening for all top infants. The SPAR Reading Test (previously the Young Group Reading Test) was given to all children in their final term in the infant department, and schools with children with a reading quotient of 85 or below qualified for a number of teaching hours provided by the remedial service. This was only a basic procedure and actually how many hours a particular school received, and exactly which pupils received what kind of help was always, at least in principle, open to a certain amount of negotiation.

The screening procedure was not unusual. Most authorities operate a similar system (Gipps *et al.*, 1983) and the type of help offered is also, for the most part, traditional in nature, but the organization of this support service was unusual. In most authorities the bulk of remedial reading help has been provided by teachers on the staff of individual primary schools. A school might be allocated an extra half of a teacher's time because of the levels of reading or other problems experienced by pupils, but once the allocation has been made, the teacher is employed at the school and is responsible to the headteacher. Where a remedial reading service and an advisory service also operate, their role is usually to encourage the head to use any remedial staff in a particular way and to provide for pupils with the most extreme or complex needs to be taught by the remedial service in withdrawal groups.

The situation in Brentonshire had always been different from this, and significantly, theirs was a system of organization that has become more common. The remedial teachers were all employed directly by the remedial service, supervised by the advisory teachers and answerable to the head of service, who was directly responsible to the adviser for special education. He, in turn, worked to the senior education officer for special education. These teachers might work in the schools but their direct superior was the advisory teacher from the remedial service, not the head of the school or schools in which they worked. This system of organization had important consequences. Because the remedial teachers were not answerable to the head of the school, they could not be used for other duties at the headteacher's discretion. In authorities where teaching staff had been cut back, part-time teachers were usually the first to go, and primary heads have reported that considerable remedial provision has been lost in this way. Even where part-time help was retained, a combination of financial economies and problems resulting from falling rolls often created a situation where the part-time teacher was the only member of staff who did not have a full-time commitment to a class.

Schools also faced additional staffing problems. In many authorities no cover was provided until the fourth day of absence. In addition, in small schools – of which there are a great many – the headteacher had a regular teaching commitment. In these circumstances it was hardly surprising that, with the best will in the world, the part-time teacher who, strictly speaking, should be used only for remedial work, in fact was constantly called upon to perform other duties. Even where schools were allocated staff specifically for remedial work, and advisers acted with vigilance to try to ensure they were used in this way, there were many instances of remedial work suffering. Because of these problems, an increasing number of authorities have come to favour the system established in Brentonshire because it ensured that the remedial work was done. It also enabled the work to be directed from the education office, thereby allowing greater control over what was done in practice.

Removing control of remedial work from the school can also bring some disadvantages, though to what extent they are actual rather than potential is less clear. There has always been a concern that any sort of arrangement that involves primary school children with special needs being taught on a regular basis by anyone other than their class teacher may result in this teacher passing over the burden of responsibility for the child, even though it is in a regular classroom that the pupil spends the majority of his or her school day. There is also a danger that remedial work becomes a distinct and isolated activity quite separate from the general business of teaching and learning in the classroom. Particularly in the post-Warnock era, with the emphasis not only on the remediation of reading problems but also on the provision of help across the whole curriculum, the dangers of this division between remedial work and other classroom activities are most evident. If there is a risk of such a separation occurring when the remedial help is given by a member of the school staff, then the danger must increase when assistance is provided by someone who is not on the school staff and whose work is directed from outside. The most extreme case of this situation is illustrated in an example given by Gipps *et al.* of an authority ('Norborough'), where the new support service was responsible not only for the assistance given to children with special needs but also for their selection. In these circumstances particularly, it would be easy for class teachers to wash their hands of the children with special needs. Nevertheless, it is not inevitable that this should happen and positive action can be taken to avoid it.

In addition to the remedial reading service, Brentonshire ran a number of other support services which are now incorporated into the SENASS and operate from the Special Educational Needs Area Resource Centres (SENARCs). These were services for the hearing impaired, the visually impaired and for the education of children other than at school – the latter having a very wide brief ranging from hospital schools to educational provision for pregnant schoolgirls and the education of travelling children. Like many other authorities, it operated no services specifically for the physically handicapped or for children with behaviour problems. Help for the physically handicapped in ordinary schools, which usually took the form of non-teaching assistance, was organized on an ad hoc basis and involved informal liaison with the area health authority. In so far as help was provided for children with emotional and behavioural difficulties and their teachers in ordinary schools, this came from the school psychological service. The staff of the new support service have a brief to provide for children with the whole range of special needs, though no new posts have been created to ensure expertise in these areas.

The school psychological service

The school psychological service in Brentonshire was a small service for the size of the authority. After 1978 there was an increase of two posts in response first to Warnock and later to the 1981 Act, and the service then consisted of a principal and ten educational psychologists. When the population of the authority and its size are considered and when, in addition, it is remembered that all the staff also contributed to the work of the child guidance service, it becomes apparent how stretched the service was. It would appear that there was never very close contact between the school psychological service and the other support services. The remedial service, which in some authorities is under the direction of the school psychological service, was responsible to the adviser for special education. The school psychological service was inevitably very much involved in the process of assessment and the writing of Statements, but it seems that its contact with the support services was still minimal and that it had not been fully drawn into the operation of the new support service. This situation, though not desirable, would appear to be not at all unusual. The relationship between the school psychological service and the advisory and support services is considered in detail in Chapter 7.

Establishing the Special Educational Needs Area Resource Centres (SENARCs)

Plans for the reorganization of support services were drawn up principally by the senior education officer and the adviser for special needs, and approved by the education committee. They were put into operation in April 1983 to coincide with the implementation of the Act. The changes were quite radical in nature, yet they involved no major staffing changes. The reorganization was based on the amalgamation of the old support services, together with a widening of their activities.

A key feature of the new service was the establishment of the Special Educational Needs Area Resource Centres. The aim was to decentralize the support services and establish centres spread throughout the county which would act as bases for all types of support staff and would take the services closer to the schools. This type of area centre is becoming an increasingly popular form of organization. Many authorities are taking the view that although some overview of provision from the central office may be desirable, there are many advantages in locating staff in places where they are easily accessible to schools, particularly in the shire counties.

Brentonshire was already divided into four administrative areas, each under an area education officer. It was decided that initially one special educational needs area resource centre would be established in each of these and a special needs team set up. Circumstances varied in terms of the number of children likely to require help, the opportunity to hasten change through being able to make new appointments and the geographical nature of the areas. It was envisaged that additional centres would be established at a later date, but that the exact form that they would take should be determined by the success or failure of the first schemes. By September 1985 the number of centres had risen to six and no radical departures had been made from the earlier plans.

To operate the four new Special Educational Needs Area Resource Centres, a new administrative structure was needed. In addition to widening the concerns of the old remedial reading service, the aim was to cater for a much broader range of difficulties and to encourage a more generalized approach to special needs as well as incorporating and preserving the specialist skills of staff in the services for the sensory impaired. A senior education officer was to have overall responsibility for the operation of the service, but after the initial establishment of the system he would not be directly or regularly involved. The administration of each centre was to be the responsibility of the area education officer, who was responsible for all types of school provision in the area. This arrangement made possible an integrated administration in which special needs provision, its staffing, planning and general organization, were considered alongside other types of provision, rather than being a self-contained enclave.

Although the area education officer had prime responsibility for the Special Educational Needs Area Resource Centre and its activities in an area, other staff concerned had additional county-wide responsibilities. The adviser for special education was concerned with the staffing and operation of all centres and was a key member of each of the area teams. In addition, there were four senior advisory teachers who had dual roles. They were each responsible for one of the centres and also for a specialism for which they held a county-wide brief, namely services for the hearing impaired and speech impaired, services for the visually impaired, the education of children not at school, and remedial provision. All these people were based at County Hall. The other staff involved were based at the centres, each centre having one or two advisory teachers who ran it on a day-to-day basis.

It is significant that at the commencement of the scheme the four senior advisory teacher posts included one for remedial work which was a post very similar to that held previously by the head of the old remedial service, but within the first two years of operation of the new service this post had been replaced by one with pre-school provision as its specialism. This change served to emphasize the distinction that the authority wished to make between the old-style remedial service and the new generic special educational needs service.

Location

One of the first tasks was to find premises in each of the areas where the special educational needs area resource centres could be based. The most important factor was the availability of spare accommodation in a suitable geographical position. Of the initial four centres, three were based in special schools. Two of these catered for pupils with moderate learning difficulties and one had widened its brief to act as an area special school. The fourth centre was based in a primary school. The various staff involved had rather different ideas about the desirability of these locations. The staff of the centre based in the primary school – and of the host school itself – were satisfied with the arrangement. The resource centre team were pleased with the accommodation and considered it appropriate to be placed in a primary school, for although they offered support to secondary schools, the bulk of their work was, and would continue to be, in the primary sector.

However, the staff of the other centres – and of the special schools in which they were based – viewed the matter rather differently. The head of the area special school was pleased that the centre had been based at his establishment. The school was housed in spacious accommodation which had originally been designed for another purpose and there was more room than the school could readily use. The school had been designated for pupils who were categorized as ESN(M); when the categories of handicap were abandoned it had become an area special school catering for children from the surrounding area with a variety of special needs, though the emphasis was still on children with moderate learning difficulties. The head saw his school as having a secure future with an expanding role to play, and the siting of the SENARC on his premises was seen by him as contributing to this development.

The advisory teacher who ran the SENARC based in this school was newly appointed to this post from outside the authority, and this perhaps aided her in the task of establishing a new type of service that brought together aspects of remedial and special education. She saw positive benefits in being based in a special school. In particular, she was able to take advantage of some of the extra support available to the special school, which was visited regularly by the medical officer, nurse, speech therapist and physiotherapist, who all attended the school on Thursday mornings to see children and parents and hold case conferences. The advisory teacher was able to establish regular contact with these professionals. This proved to be extremely valuable and particularly assisted her in offering help and advice to pupils and their teachers who had special needs that fell outside the remit of the traditional remedial service.

The situation was rather different in one of the other centres based in a special school. The centre had been accommodated there because of the school's falling roll, and the head in this instance felt that the vulnerability of his school was emphasized by having to house the centre. This led to some difficulties over accommodation when the head claimed that one of two rooms originally intended for the centre was needed, for school activities, leaving the centre very pressed for space. The head also voiced fears about the new service. He thought that it would result in a further decline in the number of children attending his school. He was of the opinion that the new service would 'persuade teachers that they could cope with children who would be far better off with us'.

The two advisory teachers based at this school also had some misgivings. Both of them had previously held posts in the remedial service, and this connection with the old regime was to some extent a disadvantage. These teachers, who had been involved in remedial work in a variety of schools and in support services in a number of authorities, had no experience at all of special education and special schools. At least at the start of the new service, they saw little if any connection between the work of the school in which their centre was based and the work they would do in the local schools.

In fact, although the relationship between centres and host special schools was very different when the centres were first established, there emerged a common pattern of virtually no professional contact between school and centre staff in either case. Even in the case where initial reactions were favourable, the type of contact that the advisory teacher saw as desirable and possible for the future took the form of the special school making use of the expertise and resources of the centre; the centre was not seen as gaining from the expertise of the special school. In fact, the main disadvantage that SENARC staff saw in being based in a special school was the possibility of being perceived as part of that school, with the consequent danger of diminished credibility in ordinary schools. Work in another area of this research project has indicated that, in fact, many ordinary schools do look to special schools for expertise in the field of special education (Jowett *et al.,* 1988), but the attitude of these advisory teachers indicates the very substantial gulf that has traditionally existed and still, to some extent, continues between remedial and special education.

The area team

Central to the concept of the Special Educational Needs Area Resource Centre is the area team. In the planning document outlining the process of establishing and operating the new system, the senior education officer for special education wrote:

> The emphasis upon the children with difficulties, however slight, in primary and secondary schools suggests a need to bring the administration much closer to the school . . . The geographical arrangements may well save travel costs, both in time and money, and, most important of all, may increase the incidence of visits to schools by members of the authority's staff. However small this increase may be, it is surely to be welcomed by the headteacher and his colleagues who face considerably enhanced responsibilities towards a child with problems. (Special Educational Needs Area Organization, 18th January 1983.)

The area teams were headed jointly by the area education officer and the adviser for special education. Each team included a senior advisory teacher who also had a county-wide brief for a specialism, the headteacher and a governor of the host school, and the advisory teachers and any other staff who might be based in the centre. The team did not include members of the school psychological service. The brief of the area team was to liaise with the school psychological service in much the same way as it liaises with health and social services. The area education officers were responsible for the preparation of Statements and the key members of the area team held case conferences to discuss assessments. They were more likely to receive written reports from educational psychologists for these meetings than to have them along in person.

The operation of the Special Educational Needs Area Resource Centres

The staffing level of each Special Educational Needs Area Resource Centre varied slightly, but four advisory teachers could be regarded as a standard staffing – comprising two generic and two specialist. The specialist staff worked in ordinary schools supporting individual children with sensory impairment who had been integrated into ordinary classrooms, and advising their teachers, but they also had a major commitment to the specialist units attached to ordinary schools. There were two main ways in which their situation changed as a result of the new organization. First, they were based in a centre and concentrated on the surrounding area, and secondly, they worked much more closely with staff outside their own specialism. Through working from the centre and being part of a team which included teachers dealing with different types of problems, they had the opportunity both to widen their own knowledge and experience and to assist the generalist advisory teachers through their own expertise.

However, it was in the role of the generalist advisory teachers that the essence of the new service lay. These advisory teachers had responsibility for the day-to-day provision of support to all types of pupils with special needs in ordinary schools, whatever the level of difficulty. This included pupils for whom Statements had been written, those with difficulties of a less severe nature and the ten per cent or so of the junior school population who had previously been the concern of the remedial reading service. Overall, this support took a variety of forms and concentrated on 1) supervising the work of the part-time staff; 2) advising schools on assessment procedures; 3) carrying out assessments both for the school and the service and for the full multi-professional assessment; 4) liaising between the schools and any agencies giving help to a pupil.

The new support service was based directly on the organization of the remedial reading service. Important features of the former system – primary schools being allocated a certain number of hours of help on the basis of the screening of top infants by reading tests, plus consultation between school and service – were in fact retained. In some instances, the service had a long-term commitment to teaching individuals or small groups of children, but in other schools their function was short-term and specific and might be a task such as the introduction of a new maths scheme for low attainers, when the support teachers would work closely with the class teachers with the backing and cooperation of the headteacher. However, they were responsible to the senior staff of the Special Educational Needs Area

Resource Centre, who had the final responsibility for deciding which schools should receive this type of help and the exact form that the assistance would take. Although these new arrangements were quite distinct from the previous ones, they retained the important feature of control being exercised from outside the school, which ensured that the level and type of support was determined by the support service, not by the school.

7 The School Psychological Service

The school psychological service has a major role to play in helping schools provide for pupils with special educational needs. In most LEAs it was the first of the support services to be established and in many cases it was also responsible for the running of other support services. The school psychological service has an involvement with the whole range of special educational needs, but educational psychologists deal principally with learning and behaviour problems. It is these special needs which are the most numerous. They are central to teachers' perceptions of special needs and are the difficulties for which class teachers in ordinary schools are most reluctant to cater (Croll and Moses, 1985).

All LEAs operate a school psychological service but there are very considerable variations in size and organization and, to some extent, function. The variations in function are closely related to the number of educational psychologists in a service: a well-staffed service can undertake work that is impossible for a smaller one. This chapter is concerned with the work which the school psychological service undertakes in ordinary schools, but it must be remembered that educational psychologists also work in the Child Guidance Service, in assessment centres, in special schools and units, with the under-fives and their parents, and with young people over the age of 16, as well as organizing and contributing to a variety of training activities.

Much of the work of the service is concerned with offering help and advice to pupils in ordinary schools, their teachers and their parents. The school psychological service also plays a crucial role in meeting the requirements of the law, as educational psychologists are required to contribute to all multi-professional assessments and to carry out reviews and re-assessments. In addition, the service is often responsible for collating all the contributions to multi-professional assessments and advising the Statementing officer on the provision that will be called for in the Statement.

Changes in staffing levels

After 1978 most authorities increased the staffing levels of their school psychological service. In part, the increase was a direct response to the requirements of the Act as the legislation explicitly required education authorities to seek the professional advice of educational psychologists in a number of procedures. There were indirect reasons too. As more attention was paid to the education of pupils with special needs, the role of the school psychological service was judged to be a critical factor in improving provision, and extra staff were also considered necessary on these grounds.

As in many other areas of special needs policy and provision, the Warnock Report was influential in persuading local authorities to move in a particular direction. The Report recommended that education authorities should aim to employ at least one educational psychologist to every 5,000 children and young people up to the age of 19. This figure had been suggested by the British Psychological Society as being the minimum required to provide a full and efficient service. The previous recommended ratio had been contained in the Summerfield Report of 1968, which had considered that one educational psychologist to 10,000 school children should be sufficient.

However, subsequent changes in the education system made it obvious that many more psychologists would be required if the potential of the service was to be fully realized. In 1971 responsibility for children previously regarded as ineducable was transferred to the LEAs; Circular 2/75 (GB. DES, 1975) brought in the SE forms procedure which gave educational psychologists a major responsibility for the ascertainment of pupils for special education; the school-age population increased with the raising of the school leaving age in 1973; and there was an increased awareness of the desirability of early intervention and prevention which resulted in more emphasis on work with the under-fives. In addition, there was an increasing number of children who displayed signs of maladjustment and who needed help from the school psychological service. All these factors increased the workload of the service before the Education Act 1981 placed yet further demands on it.

The increases in staffing of the school psychological service were very widespread, but not uniform across different authorities. Some of the largest services added to their staff substantially while some of the smallest had no increase at all. As indicated in Table 7.1, the great majority of responding authorities were employing more educational psychologists in 1984/85 than they were in 1978. In the remaining authorities, the establishment was the same although in a few cases actual staffing levels had fluctuated resulting in a short-term reduction in numbers.

Table 7.1: *Authorities with an increase in the number of educational psychologists employed since 1978*

Type of LEA	*Number of LEAs reporting an increase*	*Number of responding LEAs*	*% with increase*
County	32	36	88.8
Metropolitan	18	25	72.0
London boroughs (including ILEA)	15	16	93.8
Total	65	77	84.4

Three of the largest county authorities had services employing between 34 and 39 educational psychologists, but differences in size alone do not account for the discrepancy in staffing between these three services and those in the two county authorities which were staffed by as few as three or four educational psychologists or even the nine authorities with a service of ten or fewer. Among the metropolitan authorities, the largest service was 38 strong and the next largest were 20 and 16 respectively, while six had a staff of five or fewer. In the London boroughs, excluding ILEA, the two smallest services were composed of only four psychologists, while the two largest employed 13 and 10 respectively.

It is interesting to look not only at the total size of service but at the extent of the increases that have taken place. Table 7.2 summarizes these changes in staffing. In 1978 the average number of educational psychologists employed by a shire county authority was 12.1; by 1985 this had increased to 15.7. Similar increases took place in the metropolitan authorities where the average number rose from 8.3 to 10.0. The most substantial increases in proportional terms took place in the London boroughs: the average number of educational psychologists in post jumped from 5.6 in 1978 to 7.9 in 1984 – an increase of over 40 per cent.

Only one London borough had no increase in staff, whereas six authorities increased their school psychological service by 50 per cent or more; one service was doubled and another grew by over 90 per

Table 7.2: *Increase in number of educational psychologists employed by type of authority*

	Average number of psychologists in post 1978	1984	*Increase*	*% increase*
County N=36	12.1	15.7	3.6	29.8
Metropolitan N=25	8.3	10.0	1.7	20.1
London boroughs (excluding ILEA*) N=15	5.6	7.9	2.3	41.1

*The school psychological service in ILEA increased from 69.6 in 1978 to 84.6 in 1984, an increase of 21.4 per cent.

cent. There were also some large increases in the other authorities. Four shire counties increased their service by 50 per cent or more, as did four metropolitan authorities. On the other hand, some authorities made no changes at all or only very modest ones: one-sixth of the responding authorities maintained staffing levels unchanged, and a further one-third added only one or two psychologists to their staff.

All of these changes should be seen in the context of changes in the school-age population. Falling school rolls can mean that a stable service has, in a sense, expanded since it is dealing with fewer pupils. For the same reason, where increases have taken place, they may be bigger in real terms than the absolute figures suggest.

The school psychological service and the Education Act 1981

Prior to the implementation of the Act in 1983 the process of ascertainment for special educational treatment was in many cases the responsibility of the school psychological service. Although ascertainment, like Statementing, required a multi-disciplinary assessment, the overall responsibility was invariably in the hands of the school psychological service. This system had been in operation since 1975 when the SE forms procedure was established; previously it had been the school medical service which had been responsible for recommending pupils for special school placement. Neither the 1981 Act nor the accompanying regulations gave any special place to psychological advice as against the other professional advice that the LEAs were required to seek. This was interpreted in some quarters as an indication of an intention to allow the control and influence of the school psychological service to wane, just as the key role once played by the medical service had diminished. Other commentators have remarked upon this change: 'In the case of special education we have seen a shift from dominance by one professional group (medical) to another (educational psychology) and latterly from professionals in education to administrators' (Welton and Evans, 1986).

The introduction of the SE forms procedure established educational psychologists as the group of professionals generally in charge of admission to special education and that the influence of the medical profession in assessing educational needs diminished considerably. It is not so clear whether the 1981 Act did in practice remove the psychologists from the centre of the stage. It was certainly possible for an authority to lessen the influence of the school psychological service, but such loss of influence was not a necessary consequence of implementing of the Act.

Some authorities seized the opportunities presented by the Act to re-structure services. In cases where the school psychological service was seen as standing in the way of the implementation of an authority's special needs policy, efforts were made to curtail the influence of the service. This thinking was illustrated by an officer from a metropolitan authority who wrote in a paper on the implementation of the Act that, prior to the Warnock Report, 'it is fair to say that the school psychological service had an undue influence on the ascertainment and placement of children who were considered to require special education'. It may be that it was the decisions made by the school psychological service just as much as its position of power that were the focus of the objection. The special schools in the authority had been full, with waiting lists for places. The officer considered that too many children had been ascertained as needing special school places and that the school psychological service had been largely responsible for this undesirable state of affairs.

In response to the 1981 Act, this authority, like a small number of others, appointed a Statementing Officer to be in charge of the whole assessment and Statementing process. The following extract from the same paper outlines the key role he played and his attitude to the school psychological service.

> One person, the Statementing Officer, drafts the Statement of special educational needs. This is in contrast to some LEAs where a panel of professionals meet to compile the Statement. As a result no professional group, after submission of advice, is given a further opportunity to influence the form of the final document. For example, the educational psychologist does not have an administrative role in the procedure, but is simply one of the contributors to formal assessment.

In justification of this procedure, the officer claimed, 'It is an attempt to give equal weight to the advice provided by psychologists, teachers, doctors and others and hopefully to receive professional advice given without undue consideration of the economic or political situation.' It is central to the Act that the assessment of need should be separate from the statement of provision. This authority took the view that this was best achieved by concentrating very considerable power in the hands of one administrator.

Other commentators have seen potential dangers in this process with the administrator being more, rather than less, likely than professionals to tailor the statement to fit existing provision. On this issue Welton and Evans (1986) say: 'The ultimate decision about placement is taken by the LEA and will have resource implications for the LEA so that administrators do not want that decision to be pre-empted by professionals'.

It is of interest that Cox, a lawyer, in his discussion of assessments and Statements, assumes that it is desirable for the school psychological service to be in control of the process:

> Neither the legislation nor the regulations specify whose task it should be to collate the advice which is sought from the various specialist advisers. Many local education authorities have assumed that this should be undertaken by educational psychologists. However, some have appointed administrators to do this. Whilst this may be undesirable, there is no legal reason why this function should not be in the hands of administrators (Cox, 1985).

In many authorities it was the school psychological service which effectively became responsible for the process and procedures. It was, however, unusual for the principal educational psychologist to hold the position of Statementing Officer, so his power and influence depended on the latter supporting his recommendations. It was not unusual for the Statementing Officer (usually the assistant education officer for special education) and the principal educational psychologist to work in close collaboration, e.g. with the former drawing up the Statement but depending very heavily on the advice of the latter.

In an article describing a review of the first two years of the implementation of the Act in Derbyshire, Kramer (Area Education Officer for Special Educational Needs) spoke of 'the educational psychologist's key responsibilities: for early intervention and preventative work, for school support and pre-MPA (multi-professional assessment) work, for making the prima facie case for initiation of MPA and, subsequent to completion of the assessment, for advising the LEA on the nature, level, delivery and context of any extra resources required' (Kramer, 1985). This indicates an approach based on close collaboration between professionals and administrators. In this authority the educational psychologists were seen as the people in the best position to assess special educational needs, both directly on the basis of their own work with children and through a professional consideration of the advice submitted by the schools, doctors and other sources. It was also up to them to determine the provision that should be made available for these needs to be met.

It is worth noting that, in Derbyshire, the fact that the school psychological service exercised considerable influence did not result in high levels of special school placements. In the review of the implementation of the Act referred to above, the reactions of the teacher associations to the school psychological service indicated a considerable reluctance on the part of the latter to recommend that a child go to a special school. 'Psychologists, possibly acting under LEA instructions, seem determined to prevent the separation of children with special educational needs.' The psychologists still acted as gatekeepers to segregated special school placement but it would appear that they were not opening the gate very widely.

Section 5 of the Act specifies that where a multi-professional assessment is going to be conducted, educational, psychological and medical advice has to be sought by the authority and this can be supplemented by any other advice that the authority may consider desirable in an individual case. The advice to be sought is specified, but who is to act on behalf of the authority is not. All authorities have appointed an officer or officers to act as Statementing Officer, but the role they execute is very varied. The major difference between authorities rests on who is actually in charge of the process, irrespective of whose signature finally authorizes the documents.

Of prime importance is the decision to initiate the multi-professional assessment. There are various practices that can be used to get the assessment procedure under way. This is an area of the Act where very little guidance has been given, so that practice varies considerably. Particularly in the early days of implementation, many procedures were tried and some had unforeseen consequences. For example, one authority initially allowed headteachers to put forward, without reference to any of the advice and support services, the names of pupils on their roll whom they considered to have special needs requiring multi-professional assessments and Statements. At the same time many schools were feeling oppressed by the imposition of financial restraints and saw the implementation of the Act as a possible way of securing additional resources. To this end the heads of some large comprehensive schools put forward 20 per cent of the pupils on roll. This produced an impasse, not envisaged either by the authority or the legislators.

There are two points to be made here. First, the connection between Statements and additional resources was taken for granted, as apparently was the notion that there would be some 'surplus' resources that could be made available more generally in the school. Secondly, if schools were to be able to set the machinery for multi-professional assessments into action, some mechanism was necessary to prevent the situation described from occurring again. To this end a variety of procedures were devised, all of which involved some form of standardization of the assessment processes used in an authority's schools. Such a system of assessment was usually devised by either the school psychological service or the special educational needs advisory and support service, possibly by both in collaboration. Once such a procedure had been established, it was possible for schools to do the initial assessment of a child and, where necessary, request that a multi-professional assessment be carried out. The educational psychologist's only role in such a situation was to contribute to the multi-professional assessment. An alternative procedure was to place the responsibility for initiating the multi-professional assessment with an agency outside the school, possibly the advisory and support service but more usually the school psychological service. Under this arrangement the school was still responsible for the early stages of assessment, but instead of being empowered to call directly for a multi-professional assessment it had to approach the school psychological service, and it was the educational psychologist who decided whether a full multi-professional assessment was appropriate.

Work in schools

Besides work directly related to the implementation of the Act, the school psychological service is also concerned with assisting teachers to cater for children in their classes with a range of special educational needs who are not going to be removed for placement in special schools and who may, or may not, be the subject of Statements. Work undertaken as part of a previous DES-funded project, 'The Assessment and Incidence of Special Educational Needs' (Croll and Moses, 1985), investigated the contact that junior schools had with the school psychological service and the reactions of class teachers and heads to the help and advice that they received. The findings were based on a survey of 428 junior school class teachers and the headteachers of the 61 schools in which they taught. The schools were spread over ten LEAs of different types. The data were gathered after the 1981 Act had been passed but before it was implemented, so the psychologists were not concerned with multi-professional assessments and Statements, though of course they were concerned with ascertainment for special education. The focus of this study was teachers' reactions to the service provided by educational psychologists to help them provide for the pupils with special needs in their classes.

The headteacher was a key figure in determining the relationship between the school psychological service and the school. In over 95 per cent of the schools, all contact between the service and the school went through the headteacher. In all ten authorities it was established practice for educational psychologists always to deal with headteachers in their contact with schools and to make arrangements to see class teachers and pupils through them; there was only very rarely an opportunity for a class teacher to approach an educational psychologist directly. This system of contact could result in teachers being denied help from the service if the head of the school was not enthusiastic about using it. This was uncommon however, and only 22 teachers from the total sample of 428 claimed that their headteacher prevented them from having the amount of contact with the service that they would like. Nevertheless the head was responsible for creating, or at least strongly influencing, the disposition of the school as a whole towards the use of the service and the type and number of occasions on which it was considered appropriate for the school to seek assistance.

Although it was the head who actually contacted the service and asked for a psychologist to look at a child or discuss his or her difficulties, it was typically the class teacher who set this process in motion by recognizing the signs that a child was experiencing difficulties and deciding to consult the head. The role of the class teacher was thus extremely important as the child was unlikely to receive help from an educational psychologist unless the school contacted the service. Teachers' perceptions were particularly important in the schools where no formal testing procedures were used and the decision that a child had difficulties requiring the advice of a psychologist was based solely on the teacher's judgement.

After the head decided to consult the school psychological service, the actual procedures varied according to local practice. Just over 36 per cent of the heads said that they would contact their educational psychologist informally in the first instance and then decide on a further course of action: the majority would request the services of the psychologist in a formal way, at that time by going through the SE forms procedure. It was emphasized, both by officers and psychologists and by heads and teachers in schools, that it was both policy and practice, prior to the 1981 Act, not to refer a child to the service without parental consent nor for a psychologist to see an individual child who had not been referred. An educational psychologist might discuss a particular child and offer advice to teachers about how to cater for his or her needs without an actual referral, but would not assess the child. The services were very much orientated towards dealing with the problems of the limited number of children who were specifically referred, rather than giving advice to teachers on how best to cope with the larger numbers of pupils for whom referral would be inappropriate or offering help with general problems of classroom management and teaching. The heads of just over 72 per cent of the schools said that the contact they had with the school psychological service was always about specific children. The others had some dealings of a more general nature but they tended to take place when the psychologist was in the school to see a particular child; it was unusual for visits to be arranged where the focus was not on particular individuals.

It was extremely unusual for a head of a school not to have had contact with the school psychological service, but this was not the case with class teachers. Over 30 per cent of teachers had never had a child referred, and over half had only had a child referred once.

Just over 15 per cent of class teachers had seen an educational psychologist at some time during the school year of the research and 7.5 per cent had seen an educational psychologist that term; less than four per cent had seen an educational psychologist twice during the school year. Informal contact, outside the referral process, was much less frequent. Over 75 per cent of teachers had never consulted informally about a child and only ten per cent had had this type of contact on more than one occasion. Other types of contact were even more infrequent. Very occasionally, an educational psychologist had discussed general coping strategies with individual teachers or with a school staff. Some 13 per cent of teachers had attended in-service courses run by the school psychological service.

In outline, the picture was one of virtually all schools being in touch with the school psychological service, with the organization of this contact lying principally in the hands of the headteacher. Although most teachers had come into contact with the school psychological service, a substantial minority had not. The majority of contacts concerned individual children who had been formally referred. There was some informal consultation, again about specific children, but little contact of a more general nature.

Table 7.3 illustrates the number of children with various difficulties about whom schools sought the advice of the school psychological service. It appears that schools were more likely to ask for help in dealing with children's behaviour problems than with their learning difficulties. Schools contacted an educational psychologist about only 7.7 per cent of the children whom they considered to have learning difficulties; the corresponding figure for children considered to have behaviour problems as well as learning difficulties was 12 per cent, and for those considered to have behaviour problems only it was 13.2 per cent. This difference probably reflects teachers' desire to be rid of certain children as well as their perceived need for specialist help. Teachers were more reluctant to have maladjusted children in their classes than children with any other type of special need. They were therefore more likely to consult an educational psychologist about such a child, both because they required advice on coping with the child and because such contact would have been the first step towards removing the child from the classroom. The predominance of behaviour problems among children referred to the school psychological service was also found in a study of the service in Hampshire (Wright and Payne, 1979).

Table 7.3: *Teacher contact with the school psychological service about individual children*

Special need	*% of children considered to have special needs about whom teachers consulted an educational psychologist*		
	Referral	*Non-referral*	*Total*
Learning difficulties	4.3	3.4	7.7
Behaviour problems	6.8	6.4	13.2
Learning and behaviour	9.2	2.8	12.0
Other	0.3	0.2	0.5

There was undoubtedly a desire on the part of both heads and class teachers to see more of the service. Over half the heads and class teachers would have liked more contact with their psychologist about particular children, and 60 per cent of class teachers would have liked more help of a general nature. Rather more heads than class teachers felt that they had sufficient contact with the school psychological service about individual children (26 per cent as opposed to 19 per cent). The difference was greater when contact generally was considered: whereas 20 per cent of heads found that present contact was sufficient, only 8 per cent of class teachers found this to be the case. This difference is to be expected as the head was in control of the contacts with the service. Both heads and teachers attributed the insufficiency of contact to the fact that the educational psychologist was too busy; very few felt that the psychologists were unwilling or uncooperative.

How useful did schools find the advice offered to them by educational psychologists? Class teachers and heads were asked to rate the advice they had received and in addition heads were asked how useful they considered the psychologist's advice to be to their staff. It was apparent from their replies, as given in Table 7.4, that on the whole the heads' ratings were rather higher than those of class teachers. Nearly 40 per cent of heads considered the psychologist's advice very useful and more than 20 per cent considered it fairly useful. Only three per cent of heads thought the educational psychologist was not at all useful, as compared with 20 per cent of class teachers.

The heads expected the psychologist's advice to be appreciably less useful to the class teachers, and this in fact concurred with the teachers' views. Just under a quarter of the heads claimed that they did not know how useful their staff found the advice, which would seem to indicate an undesirable lack of communication within the school. The opinions of the rest of the heads matched the class teachers' ratings fairly closely, although there was a tendency for heads to overestimate the usefulness of advice slightly, and to underestimate teacher dissatisfaction.

Table 7.4: *The rating of the psychologists' advice by teachers and heads*

Rating of advice	*% of class teachers with experience of SPS* N = 304	*% of heads*	*Heads' rating of usefulness to class teacher* %
Very useful	20.0	39.3	23.0
Fairly useful	17.8	21.3	18.0
Neutral or mixed	13.2	11.5	0.0
Not very useful	26.0	24.6	9.8
Not at all useful	19.7	3.3	19.7
Too soon to say	3.3	–	–
No advice	–	–	4.9
Don't know	–	–	24.6

What factors determined teachers' reactions to their contacts with the school psychological service? When talking about their dealings with the service, some teachers elaborated upon particular things that they most liked or disliked. Among the teachers who gave favourable ratings overall, the factor most frequently mentioned was that the educational psychologist had given them help in the form of detailed, specific advice and materials for actually dealing with the child in the classroom. Here the teacher felt that the educational psychologist had been of positive assistance in the day-to-day business of coping in the classroom. It was the lack of such advice that other teachers pointed out most frequently as being cause for dissatisfaction. Other factors associated with a low rating were advice and/or diagnosis that only repeated what the teacher already knew, lack of feedback from the psychologist following a visit and the failure of the psychologist to consult the teacher. It would seem that failure to consult teachers and to keep them informed were real grounds for complaint though it may, at least in some instances, have been the head rather than the service that was at fault.

The other dissatisfactions expressed were more complex. It was clear that teachers often expected an educational psychologist to assess a child, identify precisely the cause of his or her difficulties and provide the teacher with a recipe to solve the problem. These were unrealistically high expectations and it is not surprising that they were often not met.

There were other factors that were associated with how favourably teachers reacted to the school psychological service. As indicated in Table 7.5, there was a marked tendency for teachers who had the most contacts with the service to rate the advice received more highly than did teachers who had less contact. Only one-third of teachers who had one contact with the educational psychologist thought the advice that they had received was either very useful or useful, and almost a half considered that the advice was either not very useful or not at all useful. In contrast, teachers who had had four or more contacts were much more satisfied: two-thirds of this group found the educational psychologist's advice useful, while only one-fifth found it not very useful, and not one single teacher found that it was not useful at all.

Table 7.5: *Rating of the usefulness of the advice given to 304 teachers by the psychologist according to the amount of contact there had been*

Rating of psychologist's advice	*Number of contacts*			
	1	*2*	*3*	*4+*
Very useful	19.4	12.3	37.5	33.3
Fairly useful	12.9	15.6	18.8	33.3
Neutral/mixed	9.7	14.9	9.4	13.9
Not very useful	25.8	25.3	28.1	19.5
Not at all useful	20.4	26.0	3.1	0.0
Too soon to tell	6.5	1.9	3.1	0.0
No response	5.3	4.0	0.0	0.0

There are a number of possible explanations for this state of affairs. It is possible that those teachers who were better disposed towards the school psychological service sought its advice more often, so the fact that the number of contacts was related to teachers' rating of educational psychologists advice could have been the result of a teacher characteristic. However, when the relationship between the desire to see more of the psychologists' and teachers' rating of their advice is considered, it appears that it was not only the teachers who rated the psychologists' advice highly that would have liked to see more of them. It can be seen from Table 7.6 that over half of the teachers who had found psychologists' advice very useful would have liked to see more of them but 36.1 per cent of this group felt that they saw enough. In contrast, 64.6 per cent of those who thought the advice was not very helpful and 60.0 per cent of those who thought it was not at all helpful wanted to see more of their educational psychologist.

So it seems that teachers were more likely to rate highly the advice received from the educational psychologist if they saw more of him or her, but wanting to see more of the psychologist was not determined by whether or not they had received useful advice in the past. The situation would not appear to have been one in which satisfaction gave rise to increased demand. There was a strong suggestion that although at current levels of provision the school psychological service found it impossible to meet demand, the number of children still waiting to be seen was not infinite. This bears out the findings of the Hampshire study (Wright and Payne, 1979).

Table 7.6: *Desire of 428 teachers to see more of the psychologist according to how useful they have found advice in the past*

Rating of EP's advice	*Percentage of teachers*			
	Like to see more	*Would not like to see more*	*See enough*	*Don't know*
Very useful	54.1	8.2	36.1	1.6
Fairly useful	57.4	15.2	25.6	1.8
Neutral or mixed	60.0	27.5	7.5	5.0
Not very useful	64.6	22.8	8.9	3.7
Not at all useful	60.0	28.3	10.0	1.7
Too soon to tell	60.0	30.0	10.0	0.0
No contact	42.7	26.7	19.8	10.8

Overall it would appear that teachers would have appreciated an increased presence of educational psychologists in schools. The teachers who had most contact with their psychologist found the service most helpful and the most common complaint among dissatisfied teachers was not seeing enough of their psychologist.

Patterns of contact

There are a variety of ways in which the school psychological service and schools come into contact. The particular arrangement in force can have a significant impact on the type of service that a school receives.

The traditional pattern of contact, which is still widespread, is the practice of the referral of individual children. This system operates on the assumption that the school will identify children who have special needs which cannot be met from within the school and that the headteacher will seek the advice of the educational psychologist. It may well be the case that the assistance of a learning support service is sought in the first instance, and the psychological service is brought in only when the situation is very serious and has been going on for some time. This circumstance can lead to schools contacting the psychological service only after they have decided that a pupil should be removed to special school, and the educational psychologist is called in merely to secure this. Secondary schools in particular are likely to act in this way. Unlike most primary schools, they do not regularly seek help and advice from the various support services. Many have their own special needs departments which aim to cater for pupils with special needs in the school, and when the assistance of the school psychological service is sought it is likely to be for the purpose of securing the removal of a pupil.

The referral of individual pupils with special needs will always play an important part in the operation of the school psychological service. Even when the predominant organizational framework is quite different, there will always be a requirement for the system to allow schools to refer individual pupils to the service. This system does however have its limitations. First, it encourages schools to use it as an 'emergency service' in the way described above, and secondly it does little to encourage early intervention or other preventive measures. It is a system that encourages educational psychologists not to seek to control the situation but to respond to existing situations. However, it must be stressed that the staffing levels of many school psychological services make any other method of operating impossible.

Where staffing levels permit, other methods of working with schools can be operated. Systems of regular visiting, often involving a contract between the service and the school, are becoming more popular. There are numerous variations to this system but they all revolve around the notion that an agreement is reached between the school psychological service and individual schools concerning the amount and type of contact that each considers to be appropriate. The result of such negotiations is likely to be the establishment of a regular pattern of visiting, allowing a different type of service to be offered. When the educational psychologist regularly visits a school, the type of service displaying the characteristics that were most appreciated by the class teachers in the survey can be developed. Much of the contact will still revolve around the special needs of individual children, but there will be the opportunity for school and service to work together on early identification with subsequent help to the class teacher in meeting the special needs identified, so that the necessity for the child to become the subject of a Statement may be averted. There will also be the opportunity for more general considerations such as the development of individual work plans and techniques of classroom management.

The school psychological service and the support and advisory service

Even in the authorities that cater most generously in the area of special educational provision, many schools could still make use of more help from both the school psychological service and the special educational needs advisory and support service. However, it is clear that there are potential hazards when help for the same pupils and teachers comes from more than one source. There undoubtedly needs to be coordination and cooperation at all levels between the different services to avoid unnecessary duplication and conflicting advice.

The Warnock Report, so frequently quoted as a source of sound policy and practice in special needs provision, appears to have been at least partly responsible for some confusion between the roles to be played by the school psychological service and the special educational needs advisory and support service.

The Report recommended the establishment of a special educational needs advisory and support service, emphasizing both the advisory aspect of the proposed service and the fact that it should be formed by the amalgamation of all the existing support services *except* the school psychological service: '. . . the school psychological service . . . would remain a separate, though complementary service' (13:3). The Report claimed to differentiate between the functions of the school psychological service and the special educational needs advisory and support service, but the following passage indicates the extent of the ambiguity that was left unresolved:

> Our proposed advisory and support service for special education will have a clear responsibility for the quality of special education wherever it takes place and will be concerned with the whole curriculum, the professional development of special education teachers, and the progress of individual children. The school psychological service, for its part, will be primarily involved in work with individual children, including assessing their special needs and making recommendations for individual programmes for them within the curriculum, and in providing support for schools and parents (13:32).

It is clear that it is the special educational needs advisory and support service, not the school psychological service, which is primarily concerned with the professional development of special education teachers and that the school psychological service has a major responsibility for assessment. But even here there is the start of some confusion. The school psychological service must be involved in Section 5 assessments, but schools have to develop and apply internal procedures to assess the needs of pupils which they themselves provide for and they must identify those pupils for whom they would like professional help in further assessment and provision. As the special educational needs advisory and support service has 'the progress of individual children' in its brief, it is left very unclear as to who should do the assessment, advisory and support work which goes on in schools before a multi-professional assessment is carried out. This ambiguity in the Report that provides the framework for much new special needs provision is reflected in current practice, where there is also a great deal of confusion.

The Warnock Report did, however, recommend that the senior adviser for special educational needs and the principal educational psychologist should work closely together and should report to the same administrative officer. This makes obvious sense, yet there are many instances where it is not the case. It is not at all unusual for the principal educational psychologist to work to the assistant education officer for special education, while the senior adviser for special education, as a member of the team of advisers, works to the senior education officer for schools. This kind of differentiation in the chain of responsibility makes working together extremely difficult.

It is in the area of work with ordinary schools that most confusion is likely to lie. Although there are a number of ways in which contact may be established and maintained, most usually the school will be responsible for contacting the services and asking for assistance. In many cases the school will be uncertain about which is the appropriate service to contact in a particular case.

Some of the problems occasioned at school level by these arrangements are illustrated in the following example. The school psychological service in a large county authority was actually part of the authority's advisory service and the principal educational psychologist was responsible to the principal inspector. He was employed on the same salary scale and with the same status as the senior inspectors, of whom there were five, one each for primary education, secondary education, in-service training, resources and further education. These five advisers plus the principal educational psychologist formed the authority's senior advisory team. There were two advisers for special educational needs but these posts were established on a grade below the senior advisers. The principal educational psychologist was of the opinion that at senior level the staff of the school psychological service and their counterparts in the advisory services had a very good working relationship. Nevertheless, he saw considerable difficulties at school level created by overlap and confusion between the two sets of staff. He saw much of the difficulty as stemming from a belief that the sole function of the school psychological service was to remove pupils from ordinary schools and secure their placement in special schools. In these circumstances when a school had a difficulty with a pupil, they were most likely, in the first instance, to call upon the special educational needs advisory and support service. If the child's problem was not acute, if the support team staff offered advice acceptable to the school and if the child was seen to progress, then there was no problem. Unfortunately, this was frequently not the case and the school's problem was not solved.

There were a number of cases where a school sought the help of a member of the support team, only to lose confidence in this help when it appeared not to work. At this point, often months after help was first sought from outside the school, the school psychological service was called in, with the school staff absolutely at the end of their tether and anxious for the child to be removed. The problem might well have been dealt with differently if the psychological service had been approached at first. The principal educational psychologist wanted the following to happen: the educational psychologist would assess the child's needs and, if appropriate, direct a support teacher to go in to offer assistance. This would in effect put the school psychological service in charge of the special educational needs advisory and support service. However, the overall trend was away from the school psychological service having responsibility for special needs support teachers.

Some of the criticisms made of the special needs support teams by the principal educational psychologist in this authority centred around the calibre of staff employed in the teams. The advisers in charge of these teams shared the view that some of the support staff were struggling. This was a general difficulty found in many authorities which reorganized their peripatetic remedial reading service into support and advisory services using basically the same staff. The schools had high expectations of the new service, which might not be met when the staff were not adequately experienced and trained to take on the wider range of responsibilities.

Many school psychological services have moved on considerably from the time when educational psychologists were primarily involved with the administration of standardized testing procedures. The extent to which services depended on these techniques has probably been exaggerated. In any case, over the last few years a far wider approach to assessment has become established. The current position is one of using standardized procedures as a strictly limited part of the approach, with assessment procedures involving a detailed analysis of skills and recommendations of courses of action closely related to the curriculum being central to the work. This type of assessment is quite different from going into a school armed with a battery of tests and pronouncing on the abilities of the child.

There is a real danger that, as the school psychological service uses fewer standardized tests, the support staff may take on this role but do it in a more limited and less informed way than the psychologists. If standardized tests are carried out in a less than rigorous way they can be very misleading. Furthermore, a fair degree of expertise is required in relating the score that a child achieves on a standardized test to what can be expected of him or her in the classroom. An inexpert interpretation of results can have damaging consequences. This particular problem over testing, although quite common, need not arise if staff from the various services have clear job descriptions, are adequately trained for the job they do and have confidence in each other's professional competence.

8 *Support Services for the Visually Impaired in Ordinary Schools*

Background

Compared with most other special needs, impaired vision is a relatively unusual disability. The fact that so few children are affected, together with the very specific requirements that they have, creates particular problems in making appropriate educational provision. As the result of a range of medical advances there has been a reduction in the number of children who are blind or have impaired vision over the last 20 years, but it is anticipated that the proportion of children affected will now remain fairly constant, at least for the time being.

Traditionally, most pupils with moderate and severe loss of vision were educated in separate special schools. Some LEAs provided such schools to cater for pupils in their own area and also for pupils from surrounding authorities, but there was also a long history of education for the visually handicapped being provided by voluntary bodies. The various schools enjoyed a very good reputation for high levels of achievement in academic and other areas of endeavour. However, as the number of pupils with visual impairment reduced, it proved impossible to keep all these schools open. The low incidence of visual impairment means that the school-age population is widely dispersed, and as a consequence many pupils can only attend an appropriate special school if they board. This is not necessarily undesirable but may be considered to have serious disadvantages both by individual pupils and their families because of the separation involved, and possibly by the local authority because of the cost.

The combination of these factors, together with the climate of opinion favouring integration and the requirements of the 1981 Act, led to more provision being made by the local authorities for the visually impaired pupils for whom they were responsible. This provision generally took the form of units attached to ordinary schools or the individual placement of pupils in ordinary schools supported by staff from a service for the visually impaired.

There were three major factors that made the creation of such provision particularly problematic. First, as pointed out by several respondents in the survey, parents did not necessarily favour integration. Some parents had reservations about their child attending an ordinary school whatever special needs they had, but this reluctance was particularly marked in the case of the parents of visually impaired children. Their main fears were for the physical safety of their children: they saw the classroom and the playground of an ordinary school as being hazardous places, as indeed they can be without proper safeguards. There was also the fear that the requisite specialist teaching, both in academic subjects and in social skills training, might not be available, or at least not available to the same standard as in a special school. Special schools were held in high esteem for the work they did in enabling children to overcome the effects of visual impairment, and parents needed to be convinced that having their child attend an ordinary school was not a second best.

Secondly, teachers in ordinary schools might be reluctant to accept pupils with visual impairment. Research has shown that class teachers in primary schools are more willing to accept pupils with a particular special need when they already have experience of providing for such a pupil (Croll and Moses, 1985). Because visual impairment is relatively uncommon, however, class teachers are unlikely to have had the requisite experience and feel that they are not equipped to teach such pupils. While there are numerous examples of the successful integration of individual visually impaired pupils, there does appear to be a very strong case for at least integrated unit provision for pupils with more serious conditions. Previous NFER studies of integrated provision indicate how successful this type of arrangement can be, both in providing the experience of an ordinary school for partially sighted and blind pupils and in building up expertise within the school (Hegarty and Pocklington, 1982).

The third factor which presented a possible difficulty in providing help from a support service rather than a special school lay in staffing the service. Teaching the visually impaired requires particular knowledge and skills, and the need for specialist training is generally recognized. Again, largely as a result of the relatively low incidence of the disability, there was a shortage of qualified staff.

However, the implementation of the 1981 Act encouraged the majority of LEAs to employ at least one qualified teacher of the blind. The Regulations associated with the Act required authorities to seek the advice of a qualified teacher of the blind when conducting a formal assessment of pupils with impaired vision. This meant that if an authority did not employ a suitable person itself, it had to acquire this service from elsewhere. The disadvantages of having to rely on 'outside' specialists were such that many authorities in fact seconded teachers already employed by them to specialist courses to prepare them to carry out the requisite duties.

The support service

The responses to the survey of support services indicate that there were a substantial minority of authorities which did not operate a specialist support service for the visually impaired in ordinary schools; of the 77 responding authorities 51 operated such a service and 26 did not. It is not perhaps surprising that it was the smaller authorities, particularly the London boroughs, which were the most likely to be without such a service.

There were several particular consequences of not having a support service for the blind and visually impaired. The probability of special school placement was increased, and this placement was likely to be extra-district and in the non-maintained sector. However, pupils could still be integrated into ordinary schools, using other methods. They might be educated in a unit attached to an ordinary school where varying degrees of integration were possible, or individual children might be integrated into their neighbourhood schools and staff appointed to deal with the particular situation. This type of 'one-off' arrangement was a very common way of responding to the needs of the physically handicapped pupil in the ordinary school but the situation was more complicated in the case of the visually impaired. The additional help required by the physically handicapped was often supplied by ancillary helpers whereas, although visually impaired pupils might benefit from the presence of non-teaching assistants, they also require specialist teaching help.

In some of the authorities that had established a generic special needs service, support for the visually impaired had become one aspect of the service. This system was operated in the authority discussed in detail in Chapter 5. It is interesting that out of the 16 responding authorities which reported operating a generic service, four did not at that time include support for the visually impaired in ordinary schools as part of the service's remit, although they did have plans to do so in the future. Three authorities operated a service for pupils with sensory impairments which offered help both to pupils with visual or hearing impairment and to their teachers. In each case the process had been one of expanding an already established service for the hearing impaired to include pupils with visual difficulties. This process involved either the employment of new, qualified staff or the secondment of existing staff to special courses.

There was a marked increase after 1978 in the number of authorities offering a support service for the visually impaired. Of the 77 responding authorities, 11 had established this type of service since 1978 either in response to the Warnock Report, in anticipation of the 1981 Act or as an aid to the implementation of the legislation. The others had operated services prior to 1978 but none had a history pre-dating the 1970s, in contrast with services for the hearing impaired and remedial services. Some of the older, established services had expanded in recent years – five had appointed extra staff since 1978. Some of the recently created services also expanded further during that period. Despite this activity the size of virtually all these services was very small; most consisted of just one qualified teacher, others had a staff of two and a very few had a staff of three or more. There was an exception to this. One metropolitan authority had a service of 18 qualified teaching staff plus technical, clerical and ancillary help.

Unlike the remedial services, where staff doing identical jobs in different authorities were on a great variety of scales, the majority of teachers in the services for the visually impaired were paid on a common scale – teachers' Scale 3. They also received the special school allowance.

There appear to be substantial advantages in having the service for visually impaired pupils as part of a generic special needs service. Most types of support work involve a good deal of individual work by those involved in it, and there is often very limited opportunity for professional contact with people doing similar work. This professional isolation is particularly acute in the case of staff supporting the visually impaired since they are so few in number and may well be the only person doing that type of work in an authority. Where there was not a generic service, the support staff for the visually impaired were most usually responsible to the officer in charge of special education or, less frequently, the adviser for special needs. The people holding these posts, especially that of education officer, were not concerned with the day-to-day operation of the service, and this could lead both to isolation and to a lack of direction in the work of the service. In a generic service, the staff of the service for the visually impaired were still the only people with their particular expertise, but they could work alongside colleagues who were also concerned with providing for pupils with special needs, even if these needs were different. They might well be working in the same schools and, on occasions, perhaps with the same pupils and teachers.

Work in the schools

In addition to information concerning the establishment and staffing of the services, more detailed information about the work done in schools was gathered from 24 services.

The distribution of time between ordinary schools and special schools and units that characterized the special educational needs support and advisory service has already been discussed. It appeared that these services retained some of the features of the remedial reading service, including an almost exclusive concentration on ordinary schools, with many services having only minimal or no contact with special schools and units. The support services for the visually impaired operated very differently. All the 24 services studied offered help to ordinary schools but this was not their major commitment. Eight of the services spent less than half their time in ordinary schools and another five divided their time approximately equally between ordinary schools and their other commitments. Only two services spent 90 per cent or more of their time in ordinary schools.

Very few of the services spent any time in special units. One service operated from a unit and had a staffing commitment to it: some 60 per cent of staff time was spent teaching in the unit. Apart from this one exception, it appeared that unit provision and the support service were generally separate from each other, at least as far as staffing was concerned. Eight other services had some commitment to special units but in most cases it was minimal, constituting five per cent or less of working time. In some cases this commitment was not to units for the visually impaired but to children in other units who had, or were suspected of having, a visual handicap in addition to their other needs.

While units for the visually impaired and the support service were, with the single exception noted above, staffed separately, the existence of unit provision could be advantageous to the support service. The advisory teacher for the visually impaired in one shire county pointed out that the creation over the previous five years of a junior and a secondary unit in addition to the previously established infant unit had made it much easier to secure materials and equipment, some of which could be used for the work of the support service.

A considerable proportion of the time of most support services for the visually impaired was spent in special schools. All 24 services had a commitment to special schools catering for a wide range of special needs, i.e. not just visual impairment. Although in some cases this was less than ten per cent of total working time, eight services spent a quarter or more of their time in special schools. The work in special schools tended to be focused on the multiply handicapped, not on those whose only difficulty was visual impairment. The need for support work in special schools emphasizes how varied special educational needs are, and the wide range of skills and resources that are needed to meet them. It is not only class and subject teachers in ordinary schools who do not have the knowledge, skills, materials and equipment to teach the visually impaired. Teachers in special schools which cater for a wide range of special needs are unlikely to be expert in the teaching of children with visual impairment, and both pupil and teacher require specialist help. Support staff in the smaller services emphasized that, although they had a commitment to both ordinary and special schools, the limited time that they had available meant that the special schools tended to miss out. Several services said that they required more staff if the needs of the multiply handicapped in special schools were to be adequately met.

Again, unlike the special needs support service, the staff of most of the support services for the visually impaired spent an appreciable amount of time on activities outside their authorities' schools and units. Activities mentioned included: work in assessment centres, eye clinics, further education establishments and nurseries; contributing to multi-professional assessments; visiting extra-district special schools; involvement with in-service training; and working with parents in their homes. Working with the under-fives and their parents was reported to be the most time-consuming of the out-of-school activities. All but three of the services were engaged in this work and regarded it as being of considerable importance.

In the ordinary schools, all of the services studied worked with both pupils and their teachers, dividing their time between them. Staff found it difficult to say exactly how much time was allocated to pupils as opposed to teachers. The pupils involved had very different requirements, and, as the number of pupils and teachers involved was usually quite small, their needs could be responded to individually. This led to considerable variation in the support provided. This was unlike most special needs support services dealing mainly with mild and specific learning difficulties which usually had a policy setting out how time was to be divided between teaching pupils and advising teachers, often with the whole emphasis of the service on either one or other activity. Despite the considerable variation between the responses made in individual cases, 21 of the 24 services felt that there was a relative consistency in practice, with five services claiming that their time was usually equally divided between pupils and teachers, four spending more time with teachers and 12 placing more emphasis on working directly with pupils.

The time that support staff from the special needs support services spent with pupils was virtually all taken up with direct teaching. In contrast, staff from the visually impaired services did little actual teaching. As one advisory teacher put it: 'There is not much time for regular teaching sessions, and the teaching that we do is usually directly concerned with visual functioning activities'. They did engage in a wide range of other activities with pupils. Much of their time was spent in assessing and monitoring pupils' sight, providing appropriate aids, training pupils in their use and monitoring their effectiveness. A wide range of aids was available: magnifiers, telescopes, reading stands, lamps, adjustable work boards, large-print books and other enlarged material, and darker lined exercise books. There were other pieces of equipment too, such as tape recorders and typewriters, which were not specifically for the visually impaired but which were particularly useful for them. Even when the actual equipment was readily available, materials such as enlarged worksheets and braille texts might not be. In some cases the support service was responsible for their production. Some of the services had technical assistants for this work.

The support staff were also concerned with teaching social skills and with counselling, an activity on which increasing emphasis is being placed. Counselling was conducted with pupils of all ages but tended to become more significant at secondary level when young people were facing adolescence and career choices. Mobility training was also seen as increasingly important as leaving school approached. Some support services conducted this training themselves, in some cases employing a mobility officer specifically for the purpose. More usually however, the role of the support service was to liaise with the social services department which provided mobility training.

Work with teachers involved explaining the nature of pupils' handicapping conditions and keeping the teachers up to date with any changes in their condition. The purpose and functioning of any aids in use had to be explained to teachers, and strategies for the day-to-day organization of classroom, playground and curriculum had to be worked out jointly. This was time consuming, both because of the individual nature of pupils' difficulties and because the class and subject teachers were unlikely to have had any previous experience of pupils with similar difficulties.

Whether the emphasis within a service was on working with teachers or pupils did not appear to be directly related to the size of the service relative to the number of pupils helped. In the case of the support services helping pupils with learning difficulties, the services with poorer staffing ratios tended to concentrate on advising teachers whereas those with better staffing ratios spent more time teaching pupils directly. In the case of services for the visually impaired, the proportion of time spent with pupils as opposed to teachers appeared to be more closely related to the other commitments of the service than to the staff–pupil ratios.

There was considerable variation in the number of pupils who were on the books of the visually impaired support services, but unlike services for pupils with mild and specific learning difficulties, all the respondents were able to say how many pupils were currently receiving help. There are several possible explanations for this. First, the vast majority of pupils with mild and specific learning difficulties are not the subject of Statements. It is the school that decides which pupils should receive assistance from the support service, and the school rather than the support service keeps the relevant records. In contrast, most though not all of the pupils on the books of the services for the visually impaired *are* the subject of Statements, so that detailed records are maintained centrally on them. Secondly, the help given by the special needs support service is usually in the form of direct teaching, which does not necessarily involve equipment or even materials directly supplied by the support service. The provision of equipment and materials *is* an essential feature of services for the visually impaired, and careful records have to be kept of which pupil has what equipment. Thirdly, there are a great many pupils in ordinary schools who have mild or specific learning difficulties. Help that a particular pupil receives, and particularly the advice that teachers receive in relation to one pupil, will generally be of use in teaching other pupils. Visual impairment is infrequent enough for this process to be unusual, so that the expertise acquired by teachers in providing for the special needs of one pupil may not be particularly relevant to other pupils.

The average number of pupils with visual impairment on the books of the services was 61, with a range from four (in one small authority) to 270. There were several reasons for this variation, over and above the varying size of the school-age population in different authorities. First, the incidence of visual handicap varied locally: it was a relatively uncommon condition and some of the administrative units were quite small, so that uneven distribution was to be expected. Secondly, authorities which were maintaining special schools for the visually impaired usually had fewer pupils in ordinary schools receiving help from the support service. Most importantly, there is the possibility that there was very considerable variation between authorities in definitions of visual impairment. The service that catered for the largest number of children was in the process of reducing both the number of support staff and the number of pupils helped. The head of the service commented that the point had been reached where the service was 'looking at kids who just wore glasses'. This is probably an extreme example, but it does highlight the difficulty of deciding who is properly a client of the service. When different services used different cut-off points, this naturally affected the number of pupils that they saw.

9 Services for the Hearing Impaired

Each of the 77 responding local authorities operated a support service for hearing impaired pupils and their teachers in ordinary schools. The integration of hearing impaired pupils into ordinary schools has a long history which preceded Warnock by many years. Of the 38 services from which more detailed information was obtained, 14 had been in operation for over 20 years, some as long as 30 years. Many others were established around the time of the reorganization of local government in 1974: although there were already support services for hearing impaired children in a number of the pre-1974 authorities, when new or vastly changed LEAs were created, new services were also established.

For all their established history, the services were definitely affected by the Warnock Report and the 1981 Act, though not as substantially as those for the visually impaired. Hearing impairment is a much more common problem and at any given time most schools have pupils who are suffering from some degree of impairment. Three of the hearing impaired services studied had been established at the time of the 1981 Act. In each case the education authority had previously used a range of provision, based on special schools and support services run by neighbouring authorities. This was an arrangement characteristic of some smaller authorities situated close to other authorities with well-established provision for the hearing impaired. The combined effects of the legislation, the desire of parents for integration and the climate of financial stringency together resulted in more authorities providing for the hearing impaired in their own mainstream schools. The Regulations associated with the 1981 Act required that when a multi-professional assessment of a pupil with impaired hearing, or suspected impaired hearing, was made, the advice of a qualified teacher of the deaf should be sought. If an education authority did not employ such a person then professional advice had to be sought from elsewhere. As hearing loss was relatively common, it was much more satisfactory for LEAs to provide their own expert advice.

In many authorities there was a tradition of placing pupils with a severe hearing loss in extra-district special schools, either on a residential basis or with daily transport, usually in taxis provided. In either case this type of provision was very expensive and not necessarily popular with pupils and parents. The last few years have seen a substantial reduction in the number of such placements. A case study of a change in provision from extra-district placement to integration into ordinary schools with the establishment of a support service was discussed in Chapter 3.

The number of hearing impaired pupils taught outside mainstream schools has decreased. Medical and surgical advances have meant a proportion of cases of hearing loss being cured, and at the same time there has been an overall decline in the school-age population, particularly at primary level. In addition, improvements in hearing-aid technology and teaching techniques enabled more pupils to be integrated into ordinary schools. Many of these children were previously educated, not in separate special schools, but in units attached to ordinary schools. As the pupils from the units were integrated into mainstream classes, unit provision became available for pupils with more severe difficulties who had previously attended extra-district special schools. There was a very strong move in this direction by LEAs, though at varying speeds. While the process was well advanced in many areas, in others it was still a plan for the future and provision for children with hearing impairment except those with more minor difficulties was still extra-district. The head of the small peripatetic service in one such area said: 'We have no units and no schools for hearing impaired pupils. About 30 children are sent out of the area to neighbouring schools and units in other authorities – most of these attend daily and are taken in taxis'.

The special unit attached to an ordinary school had been a feature of provision for the hearing impaired for some time. The organization of such provision could take a number of forms. The unit and its staff might be directly responsible to the head of the host school. Even where this was the case, the education office was likely to play a more active role than with the rest of the school. The main reasons for this were the complications surrounding the placement of pupils in unit provision, the need for careful monitoring of their hearing and educational progress and the specialist nature of the work of the unit staff. Because of these factors the unit staff, although responsible to the head of the host school on a day-to-day basis, often worked to the adviser for special educational needs or the school psychological service. In such cases, the unit provision was likely to be quite separate from the support service for the hearing impaired working with pupils individually integrated into ordinary schools.

Another system of organization was for the service to encompass both unit provision and a peripatetic support service. In these instances, of which there were many, the head of the service was also head of the unit, and the appointment carried both the salary and the responsibility of a headteacher. There were examples of authorities running services for the hearing impaired that encompassed a special school, departments in a number of ordinary schools and a peripatetic service, thus offering a wide spectrum of provision to pupils in the authority. One of many advantages of a system of this type was the relative ease with which pupils could move between the protective environment and constant specialist help of a special school, to an ordinary school with the sustained back-up of a special department supplemented by occasional peripatetic support.

Staffing the service

A comparison between the 38 services studied showed very considerable variations in staffing. The largest services were of 42 and 38 qualified teaching staff respectively, while there were seven services that consisted of just one or two peripatetic teachers. All the services were staffed by qualified teachers of the deaf, very occasionally augmented by part-time non-specialist teachers who worked in units under the supervision of specialist staff. The great variation in the number of teachers attached to the service was largely the result of the different relationships between the peripatetic service, ordinary schools and unit provision. Where the peripatetic service and units were both part of the service, then inevitably more staff were employed.

In addition to qualified teachers of the deaf and a small number of non-specialist teachers, services employed a range of other staff. Most frequently mentioned were nursery nurses. It was quite usual for a unit for the hearing impaired in a primary school to have a nursery nurse or a non-teaching assistant or possibly both. It was more unusual for nursery nurses to be permanently attached to a purely peripatetic service. There were many instances where the placement of a hearing impaired pupil in an ordinary primary school was accompanied by the appointment of a nursery nurse, but with the appointment being made on an ad hoc basis, not as a permanent feature of the support service.

Four of the services had their own audiologist, and there appeared to be a trend in this direction, though it was still more usual for audiologists to be employed by the health authority and to operate from audiology clinics. Although usually separate from the support service run by the education authority, it was essential that the audiologist worked in close collaboration with it. One authority operated a support service which, in addition to its teaching staff, also included an audiologist, two servicing technicians and three nurses or audiometricians who were all seconded by the health authority. Several services which had not yet appointed their own audiometrician mentioned that such a post might be created in the future.

One county authority had an organizational arrangement which was relatively unusual. The whole service was made up of 18 teachers of the deaf who worked on a peripatetic basis in ordinary schools, six health visitors, six nurses and a number of part-time clinical medical officers. The teachers' salaries were funded from the LEA's primary and secondary teaching budget; and the health visitors, nurses and clinical medical officers were paid for by the health authority. A single co-ordinator, whose post was financed by the education authority, was responsible for all the functions of the services (screening, diagnosis, teaching, etc.) whether they were medical or educational, and he in turn was responsible to the education officer for pupil services.

Other services had evolved and expanded, moving away from the health authority and closer to the education authority. In one London borough the peripatetic teachers of the deaf used to be attached to the hospital audiology clinic which was their base. In October 1982 they moved to vacant accommodation in one of the education authority's schools and in the following year a unit was established attached to a primary school. (This is an example of change accomplished by utilizing accommodation made available because of falling rolls.)

Despite the changes in the service outlined, the overall staffing levels in most of the 38 authorities had not changed significantly since 1978: 17 services had experienced no changes at all, 16 had increased the number of teachers employed by one or two, and only four services had grown by five or six teachers. In three instances the increase was due to the establishment or expansion of unit provision, and in the other to the appointment of three peripatetic teachers, a home liaison tutor and a tutor to work exclusively in further education. It is interesting that five authorities had actually reduced their staff in the services for the hearing impaired by between 0.5 and 3. The reason for this reduction was again claimed to be changes in unit provision. While some authorities were reducing their commitment to extra-district special school placement and were expanding their own unit provision, other authorities were a step ahead. Having already reduced or eliminated special school placements for the hearing impaired, they were integrating pupils who had previously been in special units into their neighbourhood schools and reducing their unit provision.

The staffing of the service and the level of post held by the head of the service varied according to its size and function, but when these two factors were taken into account there was much more uniformity between authorities than there was in the special needs advisory and support services. It was usually, though not invariably, the case that all teaching staff in the support services for the hearing impaired were paid the special school allowance irrespective of grade. Services that were totally peripatetic were usually headed by a Senior Teacher or a Scale 4 teacher, while those which incorporated unit work also tended to be paid as headteachers, usually Group 3S or 4S. Peripatetic advisory teachers were usually on Scale 3S, while the units were staffed by Scale 2S teachers with a few on Scale 1S.

Of particular interest were those services which did not have a head of service. Altogether ten out of the 38 services had no one on the staff who acted as head, and in some cases there were as many as ten teachers working in a service without a formally designated head. Several such teachers pointed out how unsatisfactory this was. The support services for the hearing impaired, whether or not they had their own head, were responsible to either an education officer, an adviser or the principal educational psychologist. Most frequently (in 22 cases) the service was responsible to the education officer in charge of special needs; eight services worked to the adviser for special educational needs and two to the principal educational psychologist; the remaining four worked jointly to the officer and the adviser. In support services where there was no head of service, all the staff were likely to work directly to the education officer for special needs; many services for the visually impaired were in the same position. This officer had wide-ranging responsibilities which could not include the day-to-day running of the support service; this in turn meant that the service could lack direction and find itself in an isolated position.

Some authorities had sought to solve this problem by the creation of generic services in which the activities of the various specialist services were co-ordinated and where the head of this large support service was included in major policy-making and implementation. The advantages of a generic service are many, and close contact between the various agencies and individuals catering for pupils with the whole range of special educational needs is undoubtedly desirable. Nevertheless it must be remembered that working with the hearing impaired requires particular specialist skills. The staff doing this work are trained teachers of the deaf and are not readily interchangeable with other members of a generic service.

Work with the schools

Because of the commitment of a number of services to the staffing of units for the hearing impaired, it is difficult to make any meaningful breakdown of the time the staff of the service spend in various locations. Any breakdown of the time spent in special schools, units, ordinary schools and elsewhere would relate to the total commitment of the service, not to individual staff members, and because of the commitment to unit staffing these are quite distinct from each other. Staff who worked in the units were rarely, if ever, also engaged in peripatetic work so their time was spent very differently from peripatetic staff. Nevertheless, bearing in mind that work in the units was a major characteristic of the hearing impaired support service, some interesting patterns emerged.

Thirty-two out of the 38 services studied had regular contact with special schools. The amount of time spent on this work varied considerably between services but no service committed more than a quarter of the total time available to special schools, and only three spent as much as 20 per cent in this way. More usually, service staff spent between five and ten per cent of their time in special schools. In the context of the special school, help was offered to the multiply handicapped and their teachers, not only to those with impaired hearing. In this respect, as in many others, the services for the hearing impaired and visually impaired were alike. A similar service was provided for the pupils and teachers in all kinds of special units to help with the multiply handicapped. This work in special schools and units served to emphasize both the diverse nature of special educational needs and the specialized professional help that was required to meet them. It was not only teachers in ordinary schools who required input from a support service. Teachers in special schools were also unlikely to possess all the knowledge and skills required to provide for all the special needs of all their pupils.

Each of the services had a substantial commitment to ordinary schools: this amounted to less than half of the total service time in 15 cases and exactly half in another seven. Overall, when all 38 are considered, the average percentage of time spent in ordinary schools was 50 per cent. Some of the staff who worked in the units spent a considerable proportion of their time working in ordinary classrooms. Units for the hearing impaired were almost invariably attached to, and indeed were part of, ordinary schools. Although unit staff had responsibilities and skills not shared by mainstream staff, in many instances they worked alongside their mainstream colleagues and encouraged and supported as much integration of the hearing impaired pupils into the ordinary school as possible. In this way the work of the unit teacher became much more like that of the peripatetic staff, except that the work was restricted to one school.

Like the support services for the visually impaired, a considerable amount of time was spent in activities outside school. All but nine services reported such activities. The activities listed were similar to those undertaken by the services for the visually impaired, with the emphasis on work with pre-school children and their parents, work at the homes of school-age children and their parents, and work in the audiology clinics. Other activities included: working in nurseries, colleges of further education and child development clinics; visiting extra-district schools; liaising with other agencies; and administration. One of the services offered a much more wide-ranging provision than any of the others. In addition to all the activities already mentioned, it ran classes in signing for the deaf and those who worked with them, and offered a range of services to those who became deaf later in life.

In the context of the ordinary school most services concentrated on offering help to pupils directly. Only one service spent more than half of the total time allocated to ordinary schools with teachers rather than with pupils. (This service was not particularly small but it did have a major commitment to out-of-school work, particularly with the under-fives and their parents; this cut down the amount of time available to ordinary schools.) On average, services allocated 79 per cent of their ordinary school time to pupils and 21 per cent to teachers.

Although only three services felt unable to quantify how they divided their time, others were keen to emphasize that the divisions they made were only approximate: there was considerable flexibility according to pupil need; and in arrangements such as team teaching there was no clear distinction between time given to pupils as opposed to their teachers. One service pointed out that 100 per cent of its formal commitment was to pupils but as they inevitably had also to discuss pupils with teachers this work had to be conducted out of school hours. Shortage of time for this type of liaison activity has been commented on before (Hegarty and Pocklington, 1981), but it was only mentioned once in the context of services for the hearing impaired.

For some services there appeared to be interesting variations between the type of work done in primary as opposed to secondary schools. In the primary schools, support service staff worked closely with the child's class teacher, whereas in secondary schools the concentration was very much on assistance given to individual pupils. Because of the wide range of disability encompassed by the term 'hearing impaired', pupils received very different amounts of the support service's time. Some pupils who were integrated into ordinary schools saw the support staff weekly or even more frequently, while others who were only having their hearing monitored were seen annually.

An important part of the work of the support service in ordinary schools did not involve direct teaching at all. Considerable time and care were spent in diagnostic testing and monitoring of hearing and academic achievement. Closely connected to this were the supervision and maintenance of learning aids, and the giving of advice on how to use them to optimum effect. Advice was given about placement in the classroom and techniques for measuring the handicapping effect of hearing loss. Several services were keen to emphasize the role of pastoral care and counselling in their work, which extended to careers guidance for older pupils. Many of these activities could not be carried out in the ordinary classroom and it was usual for the support service staff to withdraw the pupils they were seeing from the classroom. In fact, it was the opinion of some support service staff that tasks such as the fitting of aids and the discussion of problems were best conducted in the pupil's home and not in the school at all. Only one service claimed to see pupils only in the classroom and this was one of the few services concerned exclusively with teaching. Every other service withdrew pupils from the classroom for at least a proportion of the time that they spent in school, and 14 only saw children withdrawn from the classroom. Although the issue of withdrawal may not be as contentious for the hearing impaired as it is for pupils with learning difficulties, it is perhaps surprising that some services never saw pupils in their own classrooms.

The question of how many children in ordinary schools were currently being helped directly by the service did not elicit answers of the sort that would enable comparisons to be made between different services. Any one service would have some children on its books who were receiving substantial direct teaching from the service; others who were frequently visited; others whose progress was regularly monitored; and still more who were 'on the books' but who might well only receive annual hearing tests. Services did not appear to have a uniform practice on how they divided their efforts between these different groups. Consequently, the responses were very varied and ranged from under 20 children who were receiving substantial direct teaching in one metropolitan authority, to over 1,000 pupils in one large shire county, over half of whom were 'on the books' for monitoring. With this range of interpretation, the average number of pupils per service would be a meaningless figure. What is certain is that in one way or another a very substantial number of children were involved.

Funding

For the most part services were funded from the special education budget, as were services for the visually impaired. This was not the case in only five instances, and, even in one of these authorities, although the staffing costs formed a discrete budget, all equipment was provided from the special education budget. This would seem to indicate that by and large the support service for the hearing impaired was regarded as an aspect of special education.

10 Other Support Services

In addition to the school psychological service, special educational needs advisory and support service and services for the hearing and visually impaired, most authorities operated additional support services. Some were directly concerned with assisting ordinary schools to cater for their pupils with special educational needs, and others offered services that enabled pupils to be educated who were either not attending ordinary schools or not attending school at all.

Services for children not at school

A common arrangement was for the LEA to operate a service that had responsibility for the education of *all* children not attending school. However, there are many reasons why children do not go to school, and the various groups of children involved may have little or nothing in common with one another. In many instances they may not have special educational needs as defined by the 1981 Act, even though they require special educational provision to be made for them. Sick children form the largest group of children catered for in this way. Although some children who are long-stay patients in hospital attend hospital schools, the majority are taught by visiting peripatetic teachers. These teachers may also teach children with chronic illnesses in their homes. In most instances this provision is a short-term measure with the objective of minimizing the impact of a period away from school, and can perhaps be viewed as an attempt to prevent sick children developing special educational needs. Other children who are not at school include pupils who have been suspended, pregnant schoolgirls and sometimes the children of travellers.

Services for pre-school children with special educational needs and their parents

If children under five are assessed as having a hearing or visual impairment, they and their families are likely to become clients of the relevant specialist support service. It has already been noted that a considerable proportion of the time of many of the staff working in these services was spent in work with pre-school children and their parents.

Children with other special needs, particularly if they were severe, were also likely to be supported by a specialist service in the pre-school period. An important element in the work of this type of service was in preparing the child and parents for the child's attendance at school, and preparing the school for the arrival of the child. Many of these children had multiple and complex difficulties and would eventually attend special schools. Although the staff of special schools were used to dealing with children with severe difficulties, liaison in the pre-school period with future pupils and their parents could still be very useful to them and it was invaluable to parents.

In a smaller number of cases, children with severe difficulties might be able to attend their local primary schools, and here the pre-school support service could do important work in preparing the school to accept and provide for them. Although the service was essentially pre-school and would not continue for long after the child had started school, it could be said to support the ordinary school. Primary school teachers were, on the whole, willing to accept pupils with the whole range of special needs into their classrooms, and their enthusiasm increased with experience. The pre-school support team helped to familiarize teachers with the type of special provision required by pupils with particular special needs and offered them relevant knowledge and experience before the child arrived in the class. Without a pre-school support service or another support service taking on this role, it is difficult to see how the necessary liaison and preparatory work could be done. In principle, it is possible for the school and individual parents to arrange for this type of contact, and in isolated instances this might happen. But it is too much to expect it to happen as a general rule without the intervention of a third party with an explicit brief to promote it.

The majority of children under five who were assessed as having special educational needs came first to the notice of the health authorities rather than education. Liaison between the health and education services was therefore of prime importance and appeared to be more highly organized at the pre-school stage than in later years.

Services for the physically handicapped

Many of the children who were the concern of the pre-school support service had serious physical handicaps and, although a proportion of these children would go to special schools, others would attend their neighbourhood schools. Unlike their peers with sensory disabilities, they were unlikely to receive help from a specialist support service. Very few local authorities had traditionally operated a specialist support service for those with physical handicaps; pupils either attended special schools, and so did not need an external support service, or they attended ordinary schools where they were assisted by a variety of ad hoc measures.

Even prior to the Warnock Report and the Education Act 1981, many primary schools welcomed physically handicapped pupils. In their survey of special educational needs in junior classrooms, Croll and Moses (1985) found that many teachers had experience of teaching pupils with physical disabilities of varying degrees of severity, including pupils in wheelchairs and with other forms of restricted mobility. They also found that teachers with experience of physically handicapped pupils were almost always prepared to accept similar pupils; and that teachers with no previous experience were more willing to accept pupils with physical disabilities than pupils with other special needs.

This acceptance may in itself be a reason for the lack of systematic support. If a pupil had a marked hearing impairment, class teachers were likely to feel that both they and the pupil needed specialist help and advice. But if the pupil had a physical disability, teachers might well consider that to present no difficulties in the classroom. In some instances the pupil's difficulties were seen as solely physical and the significance of associated academic and social problems might not be appreciated. Help might be available from a variety of sources, for instance physiotherapy provided by the health authority, help from local voluntary associations and a variety of services from neighbouring special schools. In addition special equipment and materials and possibly adaptations to the building might be necessary. It was perhaps expecting too much to place the burden of the co-ordination of these services on the ordinary school, particularly the primary school, which was unlikely to have any special needs staff as such.

The most common type of help provided when a physically handicapped pupil attended an ordinary school was a non-teaching classroom assistant. This type of help was also provided, particularly at primary level, for a wide range of pupil needs. Yet there was seldom a coherent strategy about the employment and role of non-teaching assistants. Although there was considerable variation in practice, it was much more usual for the assistant to be attached directly to an individual child at a particular school, usually on a temporary basis, than to form part of a support service.

There is very little information available about the part played by non-teaching assistants in meeting special needs, though such posts are a common response to special needs. A recent piece of research into the use of non-teaching assistants in one county authority commented: 'In the county under review a very high level of ancillary help is used to meet special educational needs in mainstream primary schools. Yet no general statement clarifying the local authority's view of the ancillaries' role exists' (Robson, 1986). It was also reported that even when a Statement written for a child specified the exact number of hours of ancillary help that was needed, little if any indication was given of how the help was to be used. Heads and classroom teachers would like detailed job descriptions and guidelines about the use of ancillary help. In the absence of such guidance the class teacher and the ancillary helper were left to their own devices, and there was no guarantee that best use would be made of this additional resource.

One of the most difficult decisions had to do with the extent to which the ancillary's time should be devoted specifically to the child with special needs as opposed to being used in a more general capacity. Robson concluded from her study that the functional integration of the pupil with special needs was impeded where the ancillary's role was interpreted as directly meeting the needs of the pupil. It was in situations where the role of the ancillary was to help the teacher to meet the child's needs that the pupil was most likely to be a full member of the class. These were difficult and complex decisions to make in the classroom. It would seem that teachers did not just need support but also some direction on how to use it to best advantage.

The authorities which established a new generic special needs support service usually sought to include support for the physically handicapped within this service, either by adding these responsibilities to the duties of an existing team member or by creating a new post. The case study of this type of service in action described in Chapter 6 illustrates the advantages that can ensue from a support service taking over some responsibility for the education of physically handicapped pupils in ordinary schools.

Services for pupils with behavioural problems

There is a real difficulty in defining exactly what is meant in some areas of special educational need. At what point does a child who is rather behind his or her peers in reading skills become a child with special educational needs? When is it appropriate for a pupil with poor eyesight to be regarded as visually impaired? The demarcation line between a child who is regarded as having a learning difficulty and one who is not is essentially arbitrary. Some cut-off points may be more 'sensible' in practice than others. But wherever the line is drawn and however it is arrived at, the pupils who are next to each other on either side of the line will have more in common with each other than with children on the same side of the cut-off point but further away from it. This is most clearly seen in instances where norm-referenced tests are used as the basis for selection but also remains true when selection is based either on criterion-referenced tests or teacher opinion based on more informal techniques.

The problem of definition is most acute in the case of behaviour problems. Some measure of the confusion in this area is indicated by the number of terms in current usage – maladjusted, emotional and behavioural difficulty, disruptive, disturbed and disturbing – all in addition to 'behaviour problems'. Maladjusted tends to be a term reserved for pupils who have, or create, problems that result in special school placement. All the other terms are used as descriptions of a large group of pupils who are not flourishing in the ordinary schools which they attend. Both the types of behaviour that characterize these pupils and the perceived origins and solutions are extremely varied.

It is now widely accepted that, in general terms, the special needs of children arise from the characteristics of the child in interaction with the environment. The model of special needs arising purely because of a child's own innate characteristics (which may be amenable to amelioration or cure) has been rejected in several ways. The deficit model of special needs in which the child is seen to be lacking and at fault has been set aside along with the categories of handicap which emphasized what a child could *not* do and the ways in which he or she was defective. It has been replaced by an emphasis on what the child needs to reach his or her potential.

The concept of special educational needs is also essentially relative. A pupil is defined as having special educational needs if he or she has a greater difficulty than other pupils of the same age. Moreover, schools vary in their definitions of special need, and a move from one school to another may result in a pupil no longer being considered to have special needs, and vice versa. This variation between schools can be seen in part as a result of the characteristics that the pupils bring with them to the school but also as a consequence of how the school provides for pupils who have difficulties. A school may have few pupils with special needs because few children present difficulties or because the school offers provision of a kind that results in few pupils with difficulties developing special needs.

The issue of behaviour problems has to be set against this complex background. Definitions are very varied, and central to the difficulty is the extent to which the problem is rooted in the child or in the environment. It is important to differentiate between various types of problem behaviour, particularly behaviour that presents problems principally for the pupil and behaviour that presents problems mainly for the teacher. Croll and Moses (1985), in their study of junior classrooms, sought to make this distinction by asking teachers to differentiate between those children in their class whom they considered to have behaviour problems and those whom they considered to be discipline problems. In fact, only a very small number of pupils were regarded as presenting discipline problems in the classroom and most, though not all, of these pupils were also considered to *have* behaviour problems. The great majority of children regarded by their teachers as having behaviour problems were not regarded as being discipline problems. This was a very clear indication of junior class teachers differentiating between different types of problematic behaviour. The children most likely to be regarded as having behaviour problems were not those who were aggressive and 'acting out' but those who were withdrawn, unhappy and found it difficult to make friends. There were, in fact, three distinct groups of children: the largest consisted of children who were considered by their teachers to exhibit behaviour which caused difficulties for the children themselves; a second, very small group of children created discipline problems for their teachers but were not thought to have behaviour problems; and a third group were considered both to *have* behaviour problems and to *be* discipline problems.

No comparable research has been published that might yield similar data for secondary schools. The literature suggests that the distinctions made in the primary school, where there is a long-standing tradition of child-centred education and where children spend most of their time with one teacher, are probably not made at secondary level. In the latter, concern appears, for the most part, to be concentrated on disruptive and aggressive behaviour, absenteeism and the associated managerial problems.

There appear to be two separate, though overlapping, problems. There are children who exhibit behaviour at school that teachers consider constitutes a problem for the children themselves. As far as the smooth functioning of the classroom is concerned these difficulties could be ignored, but the solution of the children's problems is of great importance to each individual child and to the teacher concerned. There is another group of pupils, mostly of secondary school age, who, whether or not they are considered to have behaviour patterns which are problematic for themselves, present their teachers with considerable management problems. These children are frequently referred to in the literature as 'disruptive' or 'disturbing' pupils.

When primary school teachers identify children with behaviour problems, if the problem is serious enough to warrant obtaining additional help and advice, it is to the school psychological service that they are most likely to turn. Because classroom management is likely to be only one element in the problem, the emphasis is on the individual child, and in this circumstance the school psychological service is thought to be the most suitable agency. Despite the growth of the special educational needs advisory and support service and the widening of its range of activities, it is unusual for that service to include behaviour problems within its brief.

A substantial number of referrals to the school psychological service involve problem behaviour. At primary level, the educational psychologist is in a particularly advantageous position to consider the child's behaviour at school, at home and in other relevant settings; and to work, not only with the child and the teacher, but also with the child and parents. It is in this area of concern that the work of the school psychological service and that of the child guidance service most clearly overlap and need to combine.

The classroom management of pupils who exhibit disruptive behaviour tends to be viewed differently. Such pupils are more likely to be found in secondary than in primary schools. Secondary schools, as larger institutions containing their own specialist staff, have traditionally been less dependent upon the support services than primary schools and have tended to regard self-sufficiency as the normal and desirable state of affairs. Disruptive behaviour in the classroom may entail behaviour from which the individual pupil suffers but it also creates problems for teachers. The maintenance of order in the classroom is regarded as part of the professional job of being a teacher and crucial to successful teaching. For this reason, classroom and subject teachers can be reluctant to admit to failure in the classroom and senior staff reluctant to accept responsibility for disruption in the school.

There is still a certain amount of emphasis on the establishment of off-site units to provide education for 'disruptive' or 'disturbed and disturbing' pupils of secondary school age. This type of provision cannot be regarded as offering support for the ordinary school, as it seeks to solve the special needs 'problem' not by enabling the ordinary school to cope but by removing the 'problem'. (The off-site unit for 'disruptive' pupils is the only type of separate 'special' provision to which pupils can be sent without a Statement being written, and this is a practice which is open to a number of interpretations. Perhaps the fairest is to see it as a recognition that disruptive behaviour in some cases is not caused by the individual and innate pathology of the pupil concerned but by the interaction of the pupils with the environment of the school. It could be said that their school is 'failing' these young people. Nevertheless it is often far from clear how the school could change the environment it offers to particular pupils, and their presence in the school can create what at least appear to be insoluble problems. In these circumstances it is often considered appropriate for the pupil to leave the school and attend an off-site unit.)

Opinion is perhaps more divided on the issue of the education of pupils with behaviour problems in the ordinary school than on any other aspect of special education. The position of the local authorities is of course crucial in determining the type of provision made for pupils with behaviour difficulties. The Barnsley Special Education Support Team made a distinction between the different stances that authorities could take:

> Local education authorities seem to have two differing views on the treatment of disruptive children. The first suggests that it is an intrinsic part of the duty of the education services to provide for all pupils within the ordinary school, no matter what their needs and problems, and thus to direct resources to minimise difficulties; the second suggests that difficult pupils impinge upon the normal functioning of schools and that alternatives for their education should be found (BSEST, 1981).

There are complex issues in differentiating between the discipline problems of the school and the serious emotional and psychiatric disturbances experienced by some pupils. It is unlikely that most of the latter group can be adequately catered for in ordinary schools. Even in authorities where an integrationist policy had been pursued for some time, there were invariably a small number of pupils who were placed in extra-district special schools.

The off-site unit was one popular response to the problem of the education of disruptive pupils. Another strategy was the establishment of peripatetic behaviour support services; ten local authorities in the survey had established such services. Most were relatively newly formed so it seems possible that more will follow. However, the school psychological service in many authorities had been doing similar work in schools for a long time, so there was a much higher level of peripatetic support activity than was suggested by the number of behaviour support services.

The establishment of new support services and the expansion of the work of the school psychological service in this way could be seen as responses to a problem of growing concern. The number of pupils placed in special schools for the maladjusted had risen and there were widely expressed concerns about the increase in disruptive behaviour in schools. At the same time there was a greater reluctance to educate pupils with special educational needs outside the mainstream and, although there might be less enthusiasm for the integration of pupils with behaviour problems than those with other special needs, separate provision was becoming less acceptable. Of particular relevance was the belief, increasingly expressed, that the schools themselves were at least partly to blame for the problem. These factors all led in the direction of attempting to help schools to help their pupils rather than providing segregated education for some pupils.

The peripatetic support service offered a number of advantages. Many of the problems of disruptive behaviour that arose in schools were infrequent, and schools were unlikely to have the resources to deal with situations that only occurred occasionally. The support service could offer the advantage of flexible manpower. It was often helpful in situations involving disruption to obtain the view of an outsider who could view the situation impartially and take due account of the perspectives of both pupils and teachers. The operation of a support service rather than off-site unit provision also avoided the possibility of having to find pupils to fill the units once established! It has been argued that the existence of segregated provision in itself generates demand, though it would be difficult to establish the truth or otherwise of this proposition. But if schools are going to cope with all, or at least the vast majority of pupils, they most emphatically do need support in this undertaking.

It was perhaps inevitable that much of the work of a peripatetic support service still revolved around withdrawal, though it tended to be withdrawal from the class rather than from the school. Withdrawal, a contentious issue in all areas of special needs provision, is perhaps most controversial in relation to behavioural difficulties. It can, on the one hand, be regarded as desirable, if not absolutely essential, to remove pupils from a class because of the effect they have on other pupils and the teacher. This position is strongly implied in the definition of disruptive behaviour which appeared in *Aspects of Secondary Education in England* (GB. DES, 1979). Here disruptive behaviour is considered to be 'any behaviour which interferes with the learning opportunities of other pupils and imposes undue stress on teachers', and the Education Act 1981 clearly had this in mind in section 2(3)(*b*). On the other hand, it can be regarded as particularly inappropriate to withdraw a number of disruptive or disturbed pupils and put them together in a group, because they will then have no appropriate role models among their peers to help their behaviour to improve.

Behaviour that causes disruption in schools is often seen as distinct from other special needs. Teachers frequently view pupils with other special needs as suffering difficulties that are no fault of their own, and see their task as helping them to overcome their difficulties (though some may think it is the task of *other* teachers!). In marked contrast disruptive pupils are often regarded as 'wilfully bad' and beyond the limits of the teachers' normal professional responsibilities for maintaining good discipline. Primary teachers' perceptions of their pupils' behaviour problems often locate the cause of the difficulty firmly outside the school, in the children themselves and in their homes and backgrounds; the pupils are perceived as bringing problems into the school which to some extent fall outside the teacher's proper area of concern (Croll and Moses, 1985).

In opposition to this view, there is now a frequently expressed opinion that disruptive pupils should not first be punished and then, if necessary, removed from the ordinary school, because the school itself may at least have helped to cause the problem of disruption and in some cases could even perhaps be the prime cause. So instead of sympathy being with the teacher who has to cope with the 'wilfully bad', the teacher, or at least the system in which he or she operates, is to some extent seen as responsible for the problem. In these circumstances schools can be very reluctant to admit that problems exist, and this can be a major obstacle for the support service.

The head of a school psychological service which had been supporting secondary schools with disruptive pupils for some time explained how schools could come to redefine a problem. A school might have been experiencing difficulties with a pupil over a number of years: he or she might have been creating disciplinary and other management problems, and might have been attending school very irregularly. Up to a certain point, the school regards these problems as management issues and the concern of the school alone. Then quite suddenly some crisis point is reached and the whole focus of attention is changed. Instead of the problem being a management issue for the school, it becomes centred on the pupil. The child then becomes 'the problem' and the school psychological service is called in to remove the child.

This sort of redefinition can perhaps be prevented if the school psychological service or behaviour support service does not just respond to emergency referrals but has regular contact with schools. If schools sought help at an earlier stage, it might be possible for educational psychologists to help in two respects. First, they would be able to tackle the extremely difficult tasks of assessment and disentangling the management issues from the special educational needs. Different types of help could then be offered. Educational psychologists might be able to help pupils directly through counselling or by other techniques including those based on behaviour modification. They might also be of assistance in analysing relevant aspects of classroom management and school organization, and then devising, implementing and evaluating intervention programmes.

11 Summing Up

The last few years have seen a great deal of activity directed towards attempts to improve provision for children with special educational needs. Both the Warnock Report and the Education Act 1981 have made a major impact on policy and provision, but both were foreshadowed by a climate of informed opinion in favour of the type of changes recommended in the Report and required by the legislation. The process of integration in particular can be seen as an extension of the comprehensive ideal to include a group of children previously excluded from mainstream education. Although education in segregated special schools may not be the best, or even the most acceptable, form of provision for the majority of children with special needs, most if not all of these pupils do need provision beyond that normally available in ordinary schools. Simply placing children in an ordinary rather than a special school will rarely, if ever, result in their receiving the type of education they need. By definition, some form of special provision is required by these pupils, and if they do not attend a special school, then the ordinary school must ensure that it makes appropriate provision.

This is a task with which ordinary schools are not totally unfamiliar. Some 'handicapped' pupils have always been educated in ordinary schools, and many children who are eventually placed in special schools first have their special needs recognized in primary classrooms. In addition to this relatively small number of children for whom a special school placement is seen as appropriate, a much larger number of pupils with less severe difficulties have always been the responsibility of ordinary schools, though many of these in the past have not received adequate provision. The Act requires that those children with special needs who are placed in ordinary schools should receive special provision there. To accomplish this task most ordinary schools require help.

The present project has investigated some of the ways in which this help can be provided: the links that have been established between special and ordinary schools with the resultant new roles for special schools; the variety of INSET provision available to teachers of children with special educational needs both in special and ordinary schools; and the LEA response, particularly in the development and operation of support services. This volume is concerned with the last of these aspects. It has concentrated on the issues involved at local authority level in making provision for special needs in ordinary schools and examined the variety of support services operated by authorities.

All LEAs have for many years offered help to pupils and their teachers in ordinary schools through a variety of support services. Typical provision consisted of a peripatetic remedial service, a school psychological service, a service for the hearing impaired and possibly also for the visually impaired, services for the education of children not at school and sometimes other services including those for children with speech disorders and pre-school children and their parents. The number and type of services operated and the size of the different services have varied between authorities and, despite significant developments that have taken place in recent years, local variations in provision are still marked.

Altogether 66 per cent of the authorities surveyed reported that they had achieved major changes in the structure and operation of their support services since 1978, and 20 per cent had taken the step of combining certain services to form a generic service as recommended in the Warnock Report: '. . . every local education authority should re-structure and, if necessary, supplement its existing advisory staff and resources to provide effective advice and support to teachers concerned with children with special educational needs through a united support service' (13.3).

The emergence of the special educational needs advisory and support service has been a key development, albeit one taking numerous forms. In some instances it entailed little more than minor adaptations to the existing remedial service and all that really changed was the title of the service. In other instances, however, there were major changes involving the establishment of a totally new kind of organization that brought together services for the hearing and visually impaired, the physically handicapped and sick children with services for pupils with learning difficulties and other specialist provision, thereby catering for the whole range of special educational needs.

The new special educational needs advisory and support service was, however, unlikely to include the school psychological service even though educational psychologists have long been concerned with pupils with special needs in ordinary schools. There were many instances where there was considerable confusion concerning the relationship between, on the one hand, the school psychological service and the educational psychologists and, on the other, the adviser(s) for special educational needs and the staff of the special educational needs advisory and support service. There was often a lack of clear definition of the roles of the different staff involved, and it was at times unclear which activities were the responsibility of the various services. There undoubtedly needs to be coordination and cooperation at all levels between the different agencies to avoid unnecessary duplication of services to some schools and the possibility of conflicting advice.

The remedial service has been at the centre of the re-thinking and reorganization of services offering support to the ordinary school. Despite variations between authorities, the vast majority of the remedial services shared certain characteristics. First, they concentrated on reading problems and often this was their only concern. Secondly, they worked principally, and often only, in primary schools with the emphasis on the junior age groups. Thirdly, they were staffed mostly by peripatetic remedial teachers who were involved in the direct teaching of children either individually or in small groups. Fourthly, their standard method of working was to withdraw pupils from the classroom to receive extra help; usually they remained within the school but sometimes pupils would attend a reading or progress centre which might be some distance from the school.

The new services emerging are very varied but they also share a number of common features. The traditional concern with reading problems has been extended to include a wider range of learning difficulties and, in the case of the generic services, sensory impairment, physical disability and emotional and behavioural difficulties as well. The new services cover all age groups, though it is likely that there will continue to be a greater concentration on younger pupils, as primary schools, because of their smaller size, are less likely to have at their disposal all the skills necessary to meet the wide-ranging needs of all their pupils. There has been a very significant change of emphasis towards teachers as well as pupils becoming recipients of the service. This particular change in the type of help offered has significantly altered the jobs of those who work in the service and has major staffing implications.

Where help is still given direct to the pupil, there has been a move away from the practice of withdrawing pupils from the classroom in favour of the support service teacher working in the classroom with both the pupil and the class teacher. The practice of withdrawal has recently been the subject of considerable criticism, being attacked from many quarters, although not always for sound reasons. A new orthodoxy appears to have been established in which help in the classroom is seen as the only solution and withdrawal is regarded as positively undesirable. But despite strong opposition, recent research has indicated that classroom practitioners are still firmly in favour of withdrawal. Advisory and support services which wish to move away entirely from this model of support may therefore face a distinct lack of enthusiasm, if not actual opposition, from schools, and they need to be very clear about their reasons for rejecting this popular practice.

It would probably also be mistaken to encourage the pendulum to swing too far away from reading problems. Although it is right to recognize that there are a variety of learning difficulties which pupils experience and that there are means of access to the curriculum other than the printed word, reading will continue to be of the utmost importance. While other learning difficulties must be catered for, and realistic rather than impossible goals must be set for pupils, it is essential that the centrality of reading is not forgotten and that as many pupils as possible acquire reading skills.

With the emphasis changing from direct help for the pupil to support and advice for the teacher, it is difficult to gauge with any accuracy how many children are receiving help. The problems involved in measuring the influence of the service become apparent from the finding that just over 40 per cent of local authorities could not say how many children were being helped and a further 28 per cent could only give approximate figures. This uncertainty is no doubt an inevitable consequence of the style of service now being provided, but it does make any sort of assessment of its effectiveness extremely tentative.

Although the exact number of children helped is not known, it was apparent that no service aimed to reach directly all the pupils estimated to have special needs. A few of the largest services claimed to reach 10–12 per cent of the junior age group, but most catered for a very much smaller number of pupils. The only way in which the services at their current staffing levels could reach all the pupils with special needs was through advice and support given to teachers.

There are a variety of ways in which children with special needs in ordinary schools can be helped. The support services offer a type of help that has certain advantages and some possible disadvantages. Perhaps in some ideal world the class or subject teacher would be able to cater unaided for all pupils, whatever their special needs. However, in reality teachers need support if all their pupils are to receive the best possible educational provision. It is unrealistic to suppose that each school can be a self-sufficient unit that can cater for any child. The number of pupils with special needs is almost certain to fluctuate year by year. Some special needs, such as those experienced by pupils with visual impairment, are uncommon and require special expertise on the part of teachers. When support is provided by a service, rather than from the school's own staffing and resources, the specialist skills required to meet the need can be used in a flexible way to ensure that scarce resources are used to best effect and are not deflected into other channels. On the other hand, there is the possibility that when help is organized and provided from outside the school, the pupil's needs may come to be regarded as the responsibility of the support service rather than the school. The function of a support service is to *assist* the school in its task of catering for all pupils, not to act in its place.

References

BARNSLEY SPECIAL EDUCATION SUPPORT TEAM 'Team approach to disruption', South Yorkshire. (1981). *Special Education – Forward Trends* **8**, 1, 8–10.

BULLOCK REPORT. GREAT BRITAIN. DEPARTMENT OF EDUCATION AND SCIENCE (1975). *A Language for Life*. London: HMSO.

CLUNIES-ROSS, L. and WIMHURST, S. (1983). *The Right Balance: Provision for Slow Learners in Secondary Schools.* Windsor: NFER-NELSON.

COX, B. (1985). *The Law of Special Educational Needs: A Guide to the Education Act 1981.* London: Croom Helm.

CROLL, P. and MOSES, D. (1985). *One in Five: The assessment and incidence of special educational needs.* London: Routledge and Kegan Paul.

Education Act 1981 (Chapter 60) (1982). London: HMSO.

GAINS, C. and McNICHOLAS, J. (1981). 'Broader remedies', *Times Educational Supplement,* **3402**, 40.

GALLOWAY, D. (1985). *Schools, Pupils and Special Educational Needs.* London: Croom Helm.

GIPPS, C. and GROSS, H. (1986). 'Screening and identification of children with special needs in the ordinary school', *Early Child Development and Care,* **24,** Parts 1–2, 43–62.

GIPPS, C., GROSS, H. and GOLDSTEIN, H. (1987). *Warnock's Eighteen Per Cent: Children with Special Needs in the Primary School.* London: Falmer Press.

GIPPS, C., STEADMAN, S., BLACKSTONE, T. and STIERER, B. (1983). *Testing Children: Standardised Testing in Local Education Authorities and Schools.* London: Heinemann.

GOLBY, M. and GULLIVER, J.R. (1979). 'Whose remedies, whose ills?: a critical review of remedial education', *Journal of Curriculum Studies,* **11**, 2, 137–142.

GREAT BRITAIN. DEPARTMENT OF EDUCATION AND SCIENCE/WELSH OFFICE (1975). *The Discovery of Children Requiring Special Education and the Assessment of their Needs.* Circular No. 2/75. London: HMSO.

GREAT BRITAIN. DEPARTMENT OF EDUCATION AND SCIENCE (1979). *Aspects of Secondary Education in England: A Survey by HM Inspectors of Schools.* London: HMSO.

GREAT BRITAIN. DEPARTMENT OF EDUCATION AND SCIENCE (1981). *Education Act 1981.* Circular No. 8/81. London: HMSO.

GREAT BRITAIN. DEPARTMENT OF EDUCATION AND SCIENCE/DEPARTMENT OF HEALTH AND SOCIAL SECURITY (1983). *Assessments and Statements of Special Educational Needs.* Circular 1/83. (Health Circular HC (83)3: Local Authority Circular LAC (83)2).

GREAT BRITAIN. DEPARTMENT OF EDUCATION AND SCIENCE (1986). *Statistical Bulletin* 13/86. London: HMSO.

HEGARTY, S. and MOSES, D. (Eds) (1988). *Developing Expertise:* INSET *for special educational needs.* Windsor: NFER-NELSON.

HEGARTY, S. and POCKLINGTON, K. with LUCAS, D. (1981). *Educating Pupils with Special Needs in the Ordinary School.* Windsor: NFER-NELSON.

HEGARTY, S. and POCKLINGTON, K. with LUCAS, D. (1982). *Integration in Action.* Windsor: NFER-NELSON.

HODGSON, A., CLUNIES-ROSS, L. and HEGARTY, S. (1984). *Learning Together: Teaching Pupils with Special Educational Needs in the Ordinary School.* Windsor: NFER-NELSON.

JOWETT, S., HEGARTY, S. and MOSES, D. (1988). *Joining Forces: a study of links between special and ordinary schools.* Windsor: NFER-NELSON.

KRAMER, J. (1985). 'The 1981 Education Act in Derbyshire', *British Journal of Special Education,* **12**, 3, 98–101.

LYNAS, W. (1986). *Integrating the Handicapped into Ordinary Schools: A Study of Hearing-Impaired Pupils.* London: Croom Helm.

ROBSON, A. (1986). The Welfare Assistant and the '81 Act: a study of the use of ancillary helpers to maintain children with special educational needs in mainstream primary schools in H—shire. Unpublished dissertation for an Advanced Diploma in Education, Cambridge Institute of Education.

SUMMERFIELD REPORT. GREAT BRITAIN. DEPARTMENT OF EDUCATION AND SCIENCE (1968). *Psychologists in Education Services.* London: HMSO.

SWANN, W. (1985). 'Is the integration of children with special needs happening? ' *Oxford Review of Education,* **11**, 1, 3–18.

TOMLINSON, S. (1982). *A Sociology of Special Education.* London: Routledge and Kegan Paul.

WARNOCK REPORT. GREAT BRITAIN. DEPARTMENT OF EDUCATION AND SCIENCE (1978). *Special Educational Needs.* London: HMSO.

WELTON, J., WEDELL, K. and VORTRANS, G. (1982). *Meeting Special Educational Needs: The 1981 Education Act and its Implications* (Bedford Way Papers 12). Institute of Education, University of London.

WELTON, J. and EVANS, J. (1986). 'The development and implementation of special education policy: where did the 1981 Act fit in?' *Public Administration,* **64**, 2, 209–227.

WRIGHT, H.J. and PAYNE, T.A.N. (1979). Evaluation of a school psychological service. Winchester: Hampshire Education Department.

THE NFER RESEARCH LIBRARY

Titles available in the NFER Research Library

TITLE	HARDBACK *ISBN*	SOFTBACK *ISBN*
Joining Forces: a study of links between special and ordinary schools (Jowett, Hegarty, Moses)	0 7005 1179 2	0 7005 1162 8
Supporting Ordinary Schools: LEA initiatives (Moses, Hegarty, Jowett)	0 7005 1177 6	0 7005 1163 6
Developing Expertise: INSET for special educational needs (Moses and Hegarty (Eds))	0 7005 1178 4	0 7005 1164 4

Further titles report research into *Graduated Tests in Mathematics for Lower Attaining Pupils in Secondary Schools*; *Course Teams in Further Education*; *LEA Instrumental Music Provision*; *LEA Advisers* and *The Role of the Mathematics Coordinator in Primary and Middle Schools.*

Other reports based on NFER research and published by NFER-NELSON

TITLE	HARDBACK *ISBN*	SOFTBACK *ISBN*
Secondary Headship: The First Years (Weindling, Earley)	—	0 7005 1071 0
YTS: The Impact on FE (Stoney, Lines)	—	0 7005 1151 2
Choosing Schools: Parents, LEAs and the 1980 Education Act (Stillman, Maychell)	—	0 7005 1069 9
Aspects of Science Education in English Schools (Keys)	0 7005 1074 5	—
The Study of Written Composition in England and Wales (Gorman, Gubb, Price)	0 7005 1075 3	—
The Second International Mathematics Study in England and Wales (Cresswell, Gubb)	0 7005 1128 8	—

For further information contact the Customer Support Department, NFER-NELSON, Darville House, 2 Oxford Road East, Windsor, Berks SL4 1DF, England. Tel: (0753) 858961 Telex 937400 ONECOM G Ref. 24966001